how to make
someone
love you
forever!

in 90 minutes or less

how to **make someone love you forever!**

in 90 minutes or less

by Nicholas Boothman

WORKMAN PUBLISHING ■ NEW YORK

Cover design by Paul Hanson
Interior design by Elaine Tom

Cataloging-in-Publication data is available from the Library of Congress.

ISBN 0-7611-2862-X

Workman books are available at special discount when purchased
in bulk for premiums and sales promotions as well as for fund-raising
or educational use. Special editions or book excerpts also can be created
to specification. For details, contact the Special Sales Director
at the address below.

Workman Publishing Company, Inc.
708 Broadway
New York, NY 10003-9555
www.workman.com

Printed in the United States of America

First printing April 2004
10 9 8 7 6 5 4 3 2 1

"We are, each of us
angels with only one wing;
and we can only fly
by embracing one another."

—Luciano de Crescenzo

For Wendy, Joanna, Thomas, Sandy, Kate, and Pippa
Toujours l'amour!

acknowledgments

This is a simple book about a complicated subject. It could never have come into being without the cooperation of the thousands of people who let me pry into their personal world and discover how, specifically, love unfolded for them—I thank you all for your generosity.

It's one thing to write about something, another to live it. I thank my wife Wendy for her sage collaboration and my grown-up children, Joanna, Thomas, Sandy, Kate, and Pippa, for opening my eyes to more aspects of love, romance, and broken hearts than most Hollywood screenwriters could ever imagine!

I am indebted to my agent, Sheree Bykofsky, writer Megan Buckley, and my friend Amelia Thornton for inspiring me through the early drafts; to David Walker for his wit, his style, and for being there for me; Jim Gulian for keeping me on my toes and being so darn good at what he does; and to my writing coach, Marie-Lynn Hammond, for helping me breathe life and color into my words.

My gratitude goes to Stacey Alper, Suzie Bolotin, Marta Jaremko, Matt Hannafin, Paul Hanson, Bruce Harris, Jenny Mandel, David Schiller, Elaine Tom, Pat Upton, Peter and Carolan Workman, and all the lovely souls at Workman Publishing—the classiest group you could ever wish to meet— for their support, their sincerity, and their sense of humor.

Finally, my deep respect goes to my editor, Margot Herrera, for catching a thousand thoughts in flight, giving them direction, focus, and order, then letting them wing their way onto these pages.

contents

introduction
who says you can't hurry love?

C an you really kindle the flames of love in 90 minutes or less? And why 90 minutes and not 27 minutes or 6 hours? It sounds crazy and shallow—or does it? When I published my first book, *How to Make People Like You in 90 Seconds or Less*, people thought it was crazy and shallow too, until they learned that we actually decide whether or not we like people in *the first two seconds* of seeing them. By the time 90 seconds have passed, you can be well on your way to turning a first impression into a lasting relationship, be it for friendship, business, or romance. Whether they are aware of it or not, so-called socially gifted people—you know, those people who can just walk into a room full of strangers and strike up a compelling conversation with anyone—send out signals with their bodies and speak in ways that make other people immediately like, trust, and feel comfortable with them.

Once you know what they do and how they do it, you can create that kind of first impression too.

In friendship and business, this precious 90 seconds can have you off to a flying start. Given the right circumstances, with both of you sending certain signals and talking in a certain way at the right time, it can also be a prelude to love, taking you from attraction to connection to intimacy to commitment. For a small percentage of couples, these events unfold almost instantaneously, causing them to fall in love at first sight. Most couples intuitively sense the process but have to fumble their way through by trial and error before—weeks, months, or sometimes even years later— they finally click. But the process doesn't have to be so protracted—and you don't have to leave it to chance.

In order to write this book, I studied men and women all over the world as they connected and made an emotional impact on one another. I analyzed almost two thousand romantic relationships—from couples who fell in love at first sight to those who were friends for years before becoming romantically involved. I spoke to couples who'd been together for 50 years and teenagers who'd been passionately in love for a few months. I interviewed past and present partners of the same men and women to discover what they got wrong the first time, what they learned from their experiences, and how they got it right with their new partners. I even spoke to gigolos in the sunshine resorts of southern

Europe to learn their secret for making instant connections with men and women, anywhere, anytime, and without hesitation. I talked with people who had lost partners to illness or accidents, and had believed they could never love again until circumstance brought new love into their lives. I gave seminars and workshops to test the ideas in this book, and as a consequence got invited to weddings. I have known and worked with desperately insecure and physically disadvantaged folk who, miracle of miracles, found enduring romance beyond their wildest dreams even after they had given up all hope. This latter group reinforced something I have always known: There is someone for everyone and they often find each other when they least expect it.

> **Ninety minutes is as long as you'll need to look deeply enough into another person to get a strong feeling for what makes them tick—and to allow them to look deeply enough into you to do the same.**

Through all this research one thing became clear: It's not about length of time, it's about emotional progression, with each stage unfolding in precisely the right order. If you understand the architecture of falling in love, the stages involved, and how to build and choreograph them properly, it's absolutely possible for two people to fall in love in 90 minutes or less. Researcher Arthur Aron, Ph.D., found this out in a series of experiments he conducted at the University of California. A man and a woman who had never met were put in a room together for 90 minutes. They were each told that the other person was going to like them, and were instructed to exchange intimate information, such as their most embarrassing moments and how they would feel if they lost a parent. Every so often, a researcher would come in and tell them to express what they liked about each other. They were also told to gaze into each other's eyes for about two minutes without talking. At the end of the experiment, they left through separate doors. Many of the couples confessed to feeling deeply attracted and close to the other person. Indeed, the very first pair of subjects married soon after and invited Dr. Aron and his colleagues to the wedding. Conclusion: With the right person, specific body language, and mutual self-disclosure, you can bring about strong feelings of love and intimacy. Dr. Aron affirmed that the subjects' expectation that the other person was going to like them had a huge effect. "If you ask people about their experience of falling in love, over 90 percent will say that a major factor was discovering that the other person liked them," according to Dr. Aron.

Ninety minutes is as long as you'll need to look deeply into another person and get a strong feeling for what makes them tick—and to allow them to look deeply into you and do the same. If you both like and admire what you see, you can harness your mutual enthusiasm to propel the emotional progression rapidly toward unity. Not only that, if you've *really* found the right person, there's no reason why it shouldn't last forever.

My research revealed three other simple truths.

1. Falling in love and staying in love are completely separate events. Falling in love is an addictive, intoxicating, exciting, and head-spinning chemical affair. Your body is flooded with feel-good neurotransmitters like dopamine and serotonin and you're on top of the world. But staying in love is a whole different story. After the happy neurotransmitters shut down, as they inevitably will, you need something more than chemical memories to keep you together.

2. We don't fall in love with other people; we fall in love with the feelings we get when we are with them: the spiritual and emotional awakening, the lowering of inhibitions, the joy of feeling safe and warm and full of hope, the feeling of completeness—the thrill. It just sounds much better and more romantic to say, "Chris, I think I'm falling in love with you" than to admit, "When I'm with you or think about you, I get these overwhelming feelings of excitement, expansion, and longing!" We'll be discussing how these feelings can be directed and accelerated later.

Note About Point of View

Although this book is written from a heterosexual point of view, it applies equally to gay men and lesbians. The basic human requirement is the same in all loving relationships—we need to share our experiences with someone we trust and respect in order to feel complete and happy. So I ask gay readers to forgive the fact that all my examples and advice describe relationships between men and women. I defaulted to heterosexuality for simplicity's sake, but in affairs of the heart we are all the same.

3. Certain people balance us and make us feel complete socially and psychologically, while others make us feel insecure and tired, zap our self-confidence, or turn us into someone we are not. People in vibrant, long-term relationships are very aware that they complement rather than antagonize one another. They are a social and psychological team. If you end up competing or criticizing and trying to change each other after the chemistry wears off, your future together is limited.

When you meet the person who balances and completes you, the one you trust and feel comfortable with, you have found your *matched opposite*. I coined this term because it describes the way you and your partner fit together or click, and when it happens, you both know it. Being with this person is simultaneously an indescribable joy and an enormous relief. He or she will be like you in many ways but your opposite in certain key areas, and it's highly likely you'll have a happy, committed, and loving, long-term relationship. This book will show you how to find your matched opposite and tell you what to do once you have. Part 1 will help you gain a fuller understanding of yourself and who your matched opposite may be. Part 2 will show you how to fine-tune your people skills so you make a fabulous first impression and are ready to connect. Part 3 will show you how to move from connection to intimacy to love.

By now you may be wondering who I am to tell you how to make someone fall in love with you. Good question. I've been studying human behavior for the past 20 years. For the last ten I've been a Master Practitioner of Neuro-Linguistic Programming (NLP). This discipline examines how, without thinking, we use words to empower or demoralize ourselves and others.

By the time we're about 13 years old, most of us have developed fixed patterns of thinking. In fact, we have learned to think without thinking—we act and react in predictable ways. Every day we go out into the world and experience it through our five senses, then put that information into words. It's a process called *making sense,* and it goes like this:

1. You put your experiences into words.
2. Your words become thoughts.
3. Your thoughts become ideas.
4. Your ideas become actions.
5. Your actions become habits.
6. Your habits become your personality.
7. Your personality becomes your destiny.

As you get older, the same old processing patterns are still playing themselves out, but the pace has accelerated. In romance, he rejects you and whammo!—a predictable (and useless) response: "I feel bad. I'm going home to eat ice cream and watch sitcoms with the dog." Or she turns up late because she hit traffic and whammo!—a predictable (and useless) response: "I can't stand it when I'm kept waiting, dammit."

If you're unhappy with how certain aspects of your life are playing out, the best way to fix them is to make adjustments at the thinking-without-thinking level that's responsible for the problem. You've got to get back to the put-your-experiences-into-words level, a.k.a. your *self-talk,* that interior dialogue we all have with ourselves. Anything else is like putting a Band-Aid on your forehead when you have a headache. If your love life isn't happening, you can keep doing what you're doing and hope someone will turn up, or you can get to the root of the problem and make adjustments to your internal programming— looking at the cause of your dilemma (the way you're thinking) and not its effect. These adjustments will make a difference in the way you act and respond and will eventually transform your destiny. That's a small part of what you can do with NLP. As you go through this book, you'll be making quite a few adjustments to the way you think without thinking. What you choose to change is up to you.

> **If your love life isn't happening, you can keep doing what you're doing and hope someone will turn up, or you can get to the root of the problem and make adjustments.**

I earned my NLP credentials studying with the method's two founders, Drs. Richard Bandler and John Grinder, in New York, London, and Toronto. Before that I worked for 25 years as a freelance fashion and advertising photographer with studios on three continents, and founded a business consulting company called Corporate Images. What I learned both as a fashion photographer and as a student of NLP led me to write a couple of books on turning first impressions into lasting relationships—one for the social arena, one for the business world. But when it comes to this book, my best credentials are that I was lucky enough to find my matched opposite more than 30 years ago, after we had both come out of unhappy marriages.

It All Began with Kittens

As a teenager, I was the guy that almost never got the girls. Sure, I would go to dances and parties and hang out in cool coffee shops listening to all the stories, but I'd still catch the bus home alone. Fortunately, I was ambitious and I was optimistic. After a few years of lonely bumbling, I joined a rock group, learned to ride a horse, got a part-time job delivering wedding cakes to hotels. As I met more and more people, I soon figured out it's not what you think, it's the way that you think it; it's not what you say, it's the way that you say it; and it's not what you do, it's the way that you do it. Before long, I wasn't going home on that bus with the lonely hearts club band anymore. I was attracting and connecting with girls; and in my early twenties, I met a beautiful girl and married her. What I learned the hard way was that attracting and connecting is only the first step—attracting and connecting with the *right person for you* is something else.

The marriage broke up and I moved to Portugal. I opened a fashion photo studio on the top floor of a beautiful building in the heart of Lisbon. In making the rounds with my portfolio, one name seemed to crop up over and over in conversations with advertising agency people. "Do you work with Wendy's modeling agency?" "Wendy modeled for Yves Saint Laurent in Paris; she knows what she's talking about." "Wendy danced with the National Ballet, you know." "Wendy flies her own plane."

"No, I don't work with Wendy, and no, I haven't met her yet!" I replied. What's more, I was getting fed up with hearing about her everywhere I went. Before long, "Miss Perfect" was at the top of my list of people I didn't want to meet.

Then an opportunity emerged that proved irresistible to my immature sense of mischief. One of my new clients, the editor of the country's leading woman's magazine, called to ask if I would shoot the cover for an upcoming edition. It turned out not to be as glamorous an assignment as I'd hoped. It was for their annual knitting issue. She wanted a shot of three kittens sitting in a basket of wool.

"Where am I going to find three kittens?" I asked myself the moment I'd put down the phone. *Ooh, I know,* said my inner rascal. *Why don't I just call up Wonder Woman Wendy and let her take care of it?*

I tracked down her agency and dialed the phone number. The receptionist asked me to hold, and a few moments later a voice came on the other end: "Hello, this is Wendy."

"Hi. My name's Nicholas Boothman, and I'm a photographer."

"Yes, I know," she replied softly.

I went on to tell her I needed three models—kittens. I was expecting some change in her polite tone of voice but she remained gracious and calm. I pushed my luck a little further to see how she'd react. "I'll also need a small basket, some balls of colored wool, two pieces of chipboard fifty centimeters by one meter, two hinges, and some cooking foil." Most modeling agencies would tell a photographer to get stuffed if he tagged on a shopping list of props, but Wonder Woman just kept calmly saying yes after each of my requests. We finished by agreeing on a date and time.

> **I was also drifting into some kind of gravity-free zone. I couldn't take my eyes off her.**

An old wood-and-metal cage elevator serviced the historic building that housed my studio. At precisely 5 P.M. on the appointed day, I heard the motor start up and assumed one of Wendy's assistants had arrived. The elevator came to rest and a few seconds later I heard my receptionist, Cecilia, open the door. Top marks for promptness—Wendy trains her people well, I thought. (Among Portugal's myriad charms, punctuality is markedly absent.) Cecilia came in to my studio followed by the most beautiful woman I'd ever seen in my life. *Caramba! She's sent one of her models,* I thought. An orchestra in my head began playing Ravel's

Bolero as this calm, beautiful, impressive female turned to face me, leveled her bright blue eyes at mine, smiled, held out her hand, and said, "Hello, I'm Wendy."

It's hard to explain how I felt but I'll try. I seemed to lose my sense of reality; I couldn't process very well what was going on—it was like being in shock. As the orchestra upped the volume in my head a few notches, she started speaking.

"I have the kittens. You didn't ask for it, but on the way over I had them checked by a vet and he gave them a mild sedative; we'll have to wait 30 minutes for it to take effect. I brought the chipboard and the hinges. I assume you're going to make a reflector—you didn't ask for screws but I brought some. I assume you are going to glue the foil to the wood. You didn't ask for glue but I brought that too." Wow! She was right, I'd planned to make a reflector to bounce back-light onto the kittens so the direct flash wouldn't scare them. I was impressed and humbled. I was also drifting into some kind of gravity-free zone. I couldn't take my eyes off her. Yes, she was extraordinarily beautiful, but it was her general presence that was getting to me. She was so gracious.

While we waited for the kittens to mellow out, I started assembling the reflector. As I set up the shot, Wendy went to a window that looked out over the Baixa, the area of downtown Lisbon where for centuries poets, painters, and writers had gathered in coffeehouses. "I love the Baixa," I said in her direction, "it's so full of energy and romance." "Me too," she replied. I was dissolving. "Would you give me a hand?" I asked. She turned to face me and held up her palms, "Two if you'd like." She smiled again, and my heart melted.

There we were, kneeling on the floor, facing each other across the meter-long piece of chipboard. We began scrunching up the foil, Wendy from her end, me from mine, working our way toward the center. When we arrived there, our hands touched momentarily. It took my breath away. What happened next was surreal, yet I can remember it in minute detail. A rush of energy bigger and wider than anything I'd ever felt swept from my feet up through my body and out over my head straight at her. I looked directly into her eyes and I heard this voice—I know it was my own, but I didn't hear it from the inside like you normally do, I heard it from the outside—and it said, "This is the most ridiculous thing I've ever said, but I love you." The orchestra inside my head had been going like crazy, but suddenly it stopped. Wendy was looking straight at me. "Oh my God," she said. "What are we going to do now?" I knew she felt the same way. I had found my matched opposite and Wendy had found hers.

What we did do, after I completed the assignment and Cecilia took the kittens home for the night, was spend hours and hours and hours talking. We had so much to say. We shared our hopes and dreams, our opinions and experiences. We laughed at the same things, felt passionately about the same things. It was like a deep friendship set to music.

Wendy and I had much in common. She was a Brit, just like me. We were both expatriates in Portugal. She had a mischievous twinkle in her eye, just like me, and she was dressed in a stylish but low-key sort of way, which was how I fancied my own look to be. Most important, we were in similar businesses and shared a strong spirit of adventure.

But there were also aspects of her that I sensed were not like me. She had patience and a mind for detail. She was strong, solid, and private. The way she looked and listened and paid attention made me feel like I was the only person in the world who mattered.

When I got up that morning, I had no idea just a few hours later my world would be changed forever. Wendy made me understand things in ways I'd never thought of before, and I told her about places and people I'd discovered but about which she knew nothing. I felt proud and important and invincible as we laughed and shared together. She felt safe talking with me as I cherished and respected and valued her ideas. I had never been able to talk to anyone that way before; it was almost as if we'd been chasing each other around the cosmos for lifetimes and had finally come together. It was bliss. We spent the next few weeks meeting whenever we could, talking and laughing, sharing and dreaming, and just being close.

We've been together ever since. We've raised five children into adulthood and we are still nuts about each other. The way we met has stayed fresh in both our minds, and the sheer romance of it all has had a strong binding effect. Yes, we've had our tough and difficult days, but the idea of ending the relationship—of saying goodbye to the person who makes us feel complete—has never even been an option. It would be like tearing our hearts in half.

I guess it's pretty obvious to most people that Wendy and I have a strong and happy marriage. People are always asking us for our secret. In the beginning, I brushed this question off, thinking that the answer was obvious—mutual respect, common interests, attraction, etc. But as the years passed and the question kept coming over and over again, I began to realize that there might be more to it than meets the eye. So, using my NLP training, I decided to try to identify the common threads in all successful relationships, from dating through mating, and lay them out in a simple, practical, concrete way. I also wanted to show people how to make the most of their time and avoid depressing pitfalls, and help them learn from others' mistakes. How often have we heard people say, "If only I'd known then what I know now, I wouldn't have got myself into this mess"?

Specifically, I set out to

- find couples who have fallen deeply in love and stayed energized and amused with each other for a long time;

- determine what all these couples have in common and what resources they draw upon; and

• break the lessons they can teach us about meeting, connecting, and uniting with our matched opposite into a series of easy steps that anyone can follow.

The Search for the Pattern

I interviewed happy, long-term couples and others whose relationships were in various stages of disarray. I reviewed research, read books and articles on the subject, and eventually realized that almost no one was addressing something fundamental: The most successful couples embody a very delicate balance of two maxims—*like attracts like* and *opposites attract.*

There are hundreds of books about dating, flirting, playing hard to get, getting him to propose, getting her to say yes, and the like. But I was amazed at how they all seemed to miss the obvious. In the most vibrant, rewarding relationships, the people involved are matched opposites. That's what every single person hoping to find love should be seeking—a person who makes you feel whole, someone you *really* click with. There's more than one matched opposite out there for you; there are lots of them and they're all over the place. Nevertheless, most people you meet won't be your matched opposite. You'll meet plenty of people who are charming or exciting but they may not be right for you. So if you meet someone you like a lot but it's not working the way you'd hoped and you don't feel a clear sense that it's right, let the relationship go. It's not your fault, and it's not personal; it's just that you are not matched opposites.

Since my first two books were published, I've appeared on scores of television and radio talk shows and been interviewed by dozens of magazines. As a consequence, I get loads of e-mail asking for help in relationships. This book is the response to all those people who've asked me, "How do I go about finding a loving, long-term relationship?" They seem to wish someone would take their hand for a little while, tell them what to do, and guide them through the confusion to their goal. This book is for everyone who's ever felt that way. It's the best I can offer. It's got proven techniques for connecting and making a terrific first impression. It will guide you out of your nervous uncertainties and into a loving, lasting relationship. At the same time, it will demand that you be yourself and do what comes naturally. It is written from the heart and, like my other books, it's tested and it works.

So, *don't* sit back and relax. Instead, lean forward and make up your mind to act upon what you're about to read. You may or may not want someone to take you by the hand, but if you're ready and committed, all you have to do is turn the page and begin at the beginning.

PART 1
get ready

The first steps toward falling in love

are knowing yourself and finding

the person who will complete you.

1   what is love?

The Inuit people of the Arctic have dozens of words for snow, because snow in all its forms—light, heavy, powdery, drifting, and so on—is central to their day-to-day life and survival. In our culture, judging from songs, books, and movies, love is essential to our lives, and yet we have only one word for a phenomenon that's infinitely complex and varied. Love takes so many forms. There's the love we feel for our parents, our siblings, and our friends, but even setting aside this kind of familial and platonic love and focusing on romantic love—the subject of this book—there are still so many variations. Everyone has an opinion on love, but is this universal and capricious emotion capable of definition?

My dictionary says that amorous love is a deep, tender, indefinable feeling of affection and concern toward a person, such as that arising from kinship, recognition of attractive qualities, or a sense of underlying oneness. That's a good definition, as far as it goes, but love is so much more than that. It can be fleeting or enduring, tumultuous or companionable, joyous or anguished, and it changes from moment to moment, week to week, year to year.

People have been trying to understand and explain love for millennia. For me, one of the best observations about it came from the ancient Greeks. Nearly two and a half thousand years ago the philosopher Plato spoke of love in terms of completeness. In his dialogue the *Symposium* he suggested that we all search for our other half in hopes of becoming whole. He called this human desire for completeness the search for love. In the same dialogue, Plato's mentor Socrates said, "In our lover we seek and desire that which we do not have."

Every religion has its opinions on love, as love is central to our spiritual beliefs. Attend a Christian wedding and you're likely to hear what Saint Paul said to the Corinthians: "Love is patient and kind; love is not jealous or boastful; it is not arrogant or rude. Love does not insist on its own way; it is not irritable or resentful; it does not rejoice at wrong, but rejoices in the right. Love bears all things, believes all things, hopes all things, and endures all things. Love never ends."

> "Love and compassion are necessities, not luxuries. Without them humanity cannot survive."
> —The Dalai Lama

Judaism affirms that a husband and wife complete each other. According to Rabbi Harold Kushner, the Talmud teaches that a man is not complete without a wife; a woman is not complete without a husband. The Koran also espouses the notion of love creating wholeness, saying "God made man and woman to complete each other, as the night completes the day and the day completes the night." Buddhism compares love and marriage to the intermingling of emptiness and bliss. The Dalai Lama, the spiritual leader of Tibetan Buddhism, says, "Love and compassion are necessities, not luxuries. Without them humanity cannot survive."

Social scientists take a more analytical approach to understanding love. For example, Richard Rapson and Elaine Hatfield, researchers at the University of Hawaii, break love into two main types they call *passionate love* and *companionate love*. They define passionate love as a state of intense continuous longing for union with another person that involves warm sexual feelings and powerful emotional reactions. Companionate love is not as fired up. It's having tender, trusting feelings for someone. You feel deeply attached and want to commit yourself to him or her.

Robert Sternberg, a professor of psychology and education at Yale University, espouses a triangular theory of love, believing that it's made up of passion, intimacy, and commitment. Passion is the physical part—it makes you feel aroused and daring, and sometimes leads to bad decisions. Intimacy is the enjoyment you feel from being close and connected to someone, and commitment is your mutual agreement to make the relationship work. According to

Sternberg, different combinations of these three components yield different kinds of love, and when you get all three points of the triangle working together, you get everlasting love.

A More Personal View

Novelists, poets, and writers cast a different kind of light on this elusive emotion. D. H. Lawrence wrote, "Let yourself fall in love. If you haven't done so already you are wasting your life." The French novelist and romantic Marcel Proust, who is regarded as one of the great writers in the field of love, said, "Love is subjective. We do not love real people, only those whom we have created in our mind." And Antoine de Saint-Exupéry, the author of *The Little Prince,* tells us, "Life has taught us that love does not consist in gazing at each other but in looking outward together in the same direction."

No one had more to say on the subject of love than the great bard William Shakespeare. In *A Midsummer-Night's Dream* he wrote, "The course of true love never did run smooth," and in *The Two Gentlemen of Verona* he said, "Hope is a lover's staff," whereas in *As You Like It* he refers to love as madness.

You don't have to be an artist or thinker to have insight into love. When I ask the question "What is love?" at my workshops, everyone has a different response. Twenty-one-year-old Carol says, "It's butterflies in the belly and smiles all the time." Thirty-two-year-old Ryan tells us, "It's passion, strength, fear, excitement, and confusion." Forty-something Kristy says softly, "Love is knowing what the other person wants without even asking." Her friend Maggie says, "It's like a river flowing between two hearts."

Some of my favorite definitions of love come from children. When asked "What does love mean?" eight-year-old Rebecca said: "When my grandmother got arthritis, she couldn't bend over and paint her toenails anymore. So my grandfather does it for her all the time, even when his hands got arthritis too. That's love." Billy, aged four, was more poetic: "When someone loves you, the way they say your name is different. You know that your name is safe in their mouth." Passionate little eight-year-old Chris really didn't waste words on the flowery stuff: "Love is when mommy sees daddy smelly and sweaty and still says he is handsomer than Robert Redford."

The Stages of Love

The reason it's so hard to define love is that love isn't a thing you have or get like a big feather bed. Nor is it a deep warm pool that you fall into. Love is a process. It's something you do or that happens to you, and it's the emotions and physical stirrings that go along with that. The actual process of falling in love unfolds with a natural progression through four stages: *attraction, connection, intimacy,* and *commitment.* The first stage is mainly about physical attraction and is triggered by nonverbal signals we give through a combination of attitude, physique, and clothing—our overall appearance. The next three stages are mainly about mental or emotional attraction, about developing intimacy and sharing confidences. And guess what? More often than not, it all begins with a look and smile.

The first step in creating any new relationship is attraction. Without attraction, nothing happens. We humans spend our lives sizing each other up—especially when meeting strangers. It's in our nature to do so. The instant assessment we make when we first meet someone is called the *fight or flight response,* but that's a little misleading: It's really the fight, flight, or attraction response. Every new encounter represents a threat or an opportunity. We make snap judgments: Is this person a friend or an enemy, an opportunity or a threat, attractive or repellant? We each have our own ideals and preferences, many of which have been influenced by society, the media, our parents, and our peers. Some people make us feel threatened; others confused; and still others, immediately attracted. As a general rule, though, we are drawn to people we believe match our own preferences and ideals.

If two people meet and are mutually attracted, great. The way is paved for the second step toward love: connecting. Send the wrong signals or use the wrong words and the whole thing can fall apart as fast as it began, even if the potential is there. Send the right signals, say the right things, and the connection is easy and comfortable. Then it's time to move on to the next step—to create some kind of intimacy. This is where you get the person talking and keep them talking.

There are two types of intimacy, emotional and sexual. This book is primarily concerned with emotional intimacy. Other than teaching you some sexually charged flirting techniques, we'll leave your sex life to you. Emotional intimacy is achieved through both nonverbal signals, such as prolonged eye contact and incidental touching, and through a style of conversation called self-disclosure, in which you share your true self with another. As you both reveal more, you'll identify small but crucial aspects of yourselves in each other that can lead you to feelings of unity and oneness. From here the shift into commitment with your matched opposite is as natural as self-preservation itself. Indeed, it's almost the same thing. At this moment you'll know that you are no longer alone—you are complete, committed, and very much alive.

> **Send the wrong signals or use the wrong words and the whole thing can fall apart as fast as it began, even if the potential is there.**

Nobody Wants to Be Lonely

Why is having someone special so important to us human beings? Not just for companionship, for safety, or for convenience, but because we have a need to express ourselves emotionally and intellectually, we all need someone we can trust to talk to, share our experiences, and bounce our ideas off. We want someone with whom we can share life's pleasures and, most important, someone to give us feedback—to respond to what we say and let us know how we're doing. We need someone to witness us, validate us, make us feel complete.

When two people communicate openly and regularly, expressing their feelings and emotions, they give each other reassurance and hope and a connection to the future. We find all of this and more when we express ourselves in love. Scientists have proof that the emotional feedback shared between two people in love balances, regulates, and influences their vital body rhythms and keeps them healthy. Heart rate, blood pressure, hormone balance, and blood sugar absorption all are improved when two people become emotionally united in love. In other words, that old expression "They've got real chemistry" isn't merely a metaphor. People in love don't just come alive, they tend to stay alive and live richer, healthier, more exciting, and longer lives.

Looking for Love

So if love is essential to our health and well-being, why is it sometimes so hard to find? For starters, much of what Hollywood has been feeding us about the perfect partner is perfect baloney. The media, in general, have given us poor guidance when it comes to finding a person who can complete us. If you look at glossy magazines or watch TV or movies, it's easy to believe that we ought to look a certain way, smell a certain way, talk about certain things, and aspire to certain narrow financial and career objectives if we want to be in the running for a mate.

The people you see on TV and in the magazines are really just like you and me. I know, I used to photograph them. They're just regular folks except they've been coiffed, made-up, and soft-focused. They speak words written by other people, wear clothes other people choose for them, spend half their lives on diets, and sometimes undergo painful surgery. Their glamour is all part of an illusion that we've allowed to be foisted upon us. The ironic thing is, when you lift the curtain you find that all the styling, toning, and tanning doesn't add two hoots to these folks' self-esteem. Inside, they're just like everyone else.

In an attempt to meet the media's ideals, we've been hoodwinked into wearing masks and falling for others who are also wearing masks. Is it any wonder then that when the

Making Music

We've all heard the old saying "There's someone out there for everyone." And it's true. I don't care who you are, how you think, or how you look, your matched opposite is out there, waiting, looking, and longing to touch, cherish, admire, love, and complete you. You just have to find him or her—and we'll be getting to that in chapter 3.

You know that old saying about two people "making beautiful music together"? It may be corny, but it's an apt metaphor. Think of the skills I'm going to share with you as the scales you must practice in order to be able to create the ultimate Grammy-worthy, platinum-selling, Celine-Dion-eat-your-heart-out, killer love song of all time.

masks come off and we see what's behind them, we end up with a lot of incompatibility, frustration, and anger? And is it any wonder that our divorce rate is now over 50 percent?

I'm not suggesting for a minute that you let yourself go—quite the contrary—make the most of what you've got. I just want you to realize that there's nothing wrong with you if you don't look like the folks on TV and in the magazines, because they don't look like themselves either. Be yourself, maximize what you've got, and get rid of the masks. You might just find that you're hiding what you really have to offer.

We've also been conditioned to believe our prince or princess will just waltz into our lives, but most of the time it doesn't work that way. Sure, love at first sight happens (see page 32), but it's not wise to count on it. If you lost your job and just waited for someone to knock on your door and offer you a fabulous position, you might have to wait forever. You have to get yourself out there—talk to people, explore opportunities, make connections. That's where *love by design* comes in.

Love by design is a series of steps that helps you connect with your matched opposite. It's not cold or calculating and it's not settling for second best. Rather, it is understanding the process of falling in love with the *right* person and taking deliberate steps to make it happen. Love by design draws on the experiences of those who got it right and are in happy, long-term relationships, but since mistakes are often the best teachers, it also draws on those who consistently get it wrong. It uses a wealth of body language and linguistic techniques to help you make the most of your body, your personality, and your conversational abilities. You'll begin by evaluating your self-talk inner monologue and looking at the kind of person you think you are. Then you'll look at your personality traits. Are you an extrovert or an introvert? Are you rational or emotional? Are you visual, physical, kinesthetic, or auditory? Once you have a greater understanding of yourself, you can work out what kind of person you're most likely to successfully love and be loved by.

Love by Chance

Wouldn't it be great if we could fall in love with the right person at first sight? Sometimes it happens. She looks, he looks, she smiles, he smiles—suddenly passions are stirred, inhibitions discarded, and whammo!—love at first sight. This kind of love occurs when two people immediately recognize something in each other that they absolutely know they want. The attraction is so profound that it compels them to act—in fact, it's usually so strong that all caution and common sense go out the window.

Research shows that it's not just a physical, sexual attraction, but rather the mutual recognition that you also complement each other perfectly in terms of personality and temperament.

Dr. Earl Naumann, author of *Love at First Sight,* interviewed and surveyed 1,500 individuals of all races, religions, and backgrounds across America, and concluded that love at first sight is not a rare experience. What's more, Dr. Naumann theorizes that if you believe in love at first sight, there's a roughly 60 percent chance it will happen to you. Here's what led him to that conclusion:

• Nearly two thirds of the population believes in love at first sight.

- Of the believers, more than half have experienced it.
- Fifty-five percent of those who experienced it married the object of their affection.
- Three quarters of these married couples stayed married.

Take the story of Francis and Eileen, the parents of two of my closest friends. During the Second World War, Francis was a Spitfire pilot, and one night he attended a theatrical review for the troops. "The moment Eileen stepped onto the stage, the strangest feeling came over me," Francis told me. "I thought, *That's my wife*. I had not a single doubt in my mind. I had no idea who she was but I knew this woman would be with me for the rest of my life. When the show was over, I went backstage and wangled an introduction. Our eyes locked and I felt an enormous surge of love and it took my breath away. I remember thinking that that single moment was worth my whole life."

Francis and Eileen have been married now for 48 years and have two children and five grandchildren. Interestingly, many years later their son Martin, now a successful businessman, was sitting in a bar in Chicago when in walked three female flight attendants. "Time stood still," he told me. "I turned to a colleague and said, 'That's my wife.'" He was right. Now, 24 years later, they have three beautiful teenage children.

EXERCISE

Who Are You? What Are You Like?

Take a few minutes to consider the following questions about how you see yourself, how you think others see you, and what qualities you consider important in others.

1. What five words would you use to describe yourself?
2. What five words do you think others would use to describe you?
3. Are the words similar? If not, why do you think there is a difference?
4. With the exception of commenting on your looks, what is the best compliment someone could give you?
5. What do you believe are the three most important qualities for a friend to have? A business partner? A romantic partner?

When you know what you're looking for, you can fine-tune your *self-presentation* so that you make a fabulous first impression. You can optimize your *rapport skills* to accelerate your ability to connect with someone and find common ground. From there, you can glide rapidly into intimacy by *self-disclosure,* sharing the kind of confidential information that creates bonds between people. I'll teach you to manage the timing, risk, and excitement in all of this so you can move through the steps as effectively as possible.

who will complete you?

Imagine you had to spend the rest of your life in a rowboat. It's a wide boat, so it takes two at the oars to keep the boat going forward. You and the other rower would need to agree on a direction, row at the same rhythm and speed, and be content to stay on your side of the boat—otherwise you'd go around in circles until you went nuts. Given all this, no doubt you'd be very selective about whom you chose for a partner.

That boat is a loving relationship, and not just anyone will do to help you row it. For starters you need to find someone headed the same way you are, someone whom you can get along with and who at the same time can fill you with enthusiasm when the effort of making the journey seems too hard. There will be plenty of give and take, plenty of times when you have to keep each other amused, endure some moaning and groaning, cheer each other up, calm each other down, keep each other safe, weather a storm, bask in the sunshine, make friends along the way, look out for each other, and make room for passengers. With so much riding on your choice, you'll probably have to consider a few partners before you find the right one.

You are going to grow together as you row together, matching each other stroke for stroke (more or less) but from opposite sides of the boat. The partner you choose should be able to make the trip interesting, opening your eyes to new thoughts, ideas, and horizons as you go along. You need to find someone who understands you and complements you, someone who's like you in some ways but different in others. You need to find your matched opposite and make him or her fall in love with you.

The Key to the Heart

Early on in my workshops I ask the participants, "So, how do you make someone fall in love with you?" The range of replies is as varied as the definitions of love we saw in the last chapter.

One twenty-something said, "You take her up a roller coaster to get her excited, then tell her you want to be her boyfriend."

"Does it work?" I asked.

"No," he said, "but I read somewhere that it's supposed to."

An attractive thirty-something young woman said, "I just don't hold back. I make a move on the men I'm attracted to."

"Does it work?"

"No," she admitted. "I keep making a fool of myself."

Another handsome, impeccably dressed young guy confessed, "Let her know how wealthy you are."

"Does it work?"

"Sure," he answered, "if you go for gold diggers."

A dark-haired woman in her late twenties said, "I'm friendly and open, but all that happens is I end up making friends with lots of people like me."

A good-looking guy with a strong Australian accent said, "I play hot and cold with them. All flowers and romance one day, then I don't answer her calls for a week. Then all over her again like she is the only woman in the world."

"Does it work?"

"Yes and no. Depends what you call two screwed up marriages."

The fact is, most of us are relatively clueless about how to find love, and as a result we go about looking in a pretty haphazard way. We're so convinced that love is supposed to just happen—like it does in the movies—that we mostly rely on chance. But as in the rest of life, you have a much better chance of finding something when you know what you're looking for.

The Principle of Completion

When we hear people in strong, fun-filled, productive, and lasting relationships say things like, "She makes me feel whole," or, "We just feel right for each other," they're all getting at the same thing: Both partners bring to the relationship qualities the other lacks, and together they feel like more than the sum of their parts. These couples are telling us that they are complementary psychological opposites, and it's this oppositeness that's critical to the success of their relationships. Remember what Socrates said in the last chapter: "In our lover we seek and desire that which we do not have."

Most friendships are based on the fact that we like people who are like us: Birds of a feather flock together. Obviously our friends aren't our clones—we may differ from our buddies in many ways—but at the core usually we do share quite a lot in common, whether it's values, hobbies, traditions, political beliefs, cultural backgrounds, or what have you. Generally, the more we have in common, the better we get along.

That same element of commonality is a requirement in romantic relationships. You see it all around you—outdoor types favor outdoor types, intellectuals choose intellectuals, the rich and famous hobnob with their own kind, and on and on. We find comfort in familiarity. The more you have in common with someone, the more comfortable and trusting you tend to feel. In the long run it's far easier to coexist harmoniously with someone with whom you share beliefs and goals regarding money, achievement, child rearing, and the like. Hollywood's depictions of millionaires marrying chambermaids and living happily ever after are romantic and fun to watch, but if it's lasting love you're after, it ain't so easy.

Familiarity and friendship aren't enough to sustain a romantic relationship, though. It takes something more, a whole extra dimension, one that leads to expansion, growth, and vibrancy. That's where the opposite comes in.

People with different personality types complement each other. For example, if you are an impulsive, assertive type, you may do best with someone who is more laid-back, but who in turn is energized by

> **Familiarity and friendship aren't enough to sustain a romantic relationship. It takes something more.**

your get-up-and-go. Let's take a look at how it worked in one real-life situation.

Alan is a bright, good-looking human resources VP in his early thirties, whom I met at one of my workshops a couple of years back. He is ready to marry and start a family. He dated a string of stylish, good-looking women with great careers (one was a radio host, another managed a software company), but even though he was always enthusiastic at the start, the relationships seemed to fizzle out after a few months. Then Alan met Sarah. Sarah is pretty enough, Alan's

Mere Opposites

All our lives we've heard that opposites attract. But do they really? The short answer is, "Occasionally." Sometimes we may find ourselves attracted to someone who seems nothing like us—they may be far younger or older, more free-spirited or responsible—but chances are it won't be long before one or both of us decides to jump ship, leaving the other to row in circles again.

Often these relationships take place at a time of transition in our lives, a time when, for whatever reason, we may want to break out of our old patterns. For a while we may find delight in the contrast. Responsible types may get a thrill by edging up against the wild side, while dyed-in-the-wool bohemians may feel comforted by the straight and narrow. As the relationship develops, though, we often begin to see our mate's differences as flaws that need fixing, and try to mold them into who we think they should be—which is usually someone more like us.

friends noted, but not like the knockouts he usually dated. Her job isn't particularly glamorous or high-powered either; she's the assistant manager for a local hotel.

And yet, Alan said, "Sarah made me feel special from the first time I met her. Her car broke down ahead of me at a busy intersection, and I got out to help her. She was really appreciative." He laughed. "My other girlfriends would probably have told me to mind my own business, that they could deal with it themselves."

Alan soon learned that no matter what he and Sarah were doing together, she made him feel energized and in charge in a subtle way, which was something he hadn't felt with the other women he'd dated. They had professed love for him, but he'd always felt that on some level they were competing with him, even in trivial things. Something different was going on with Sarah, and he was falling in love more deeply than he ever had before. "It sounds odd, but it's as if we were made for each other."

"What is it about Sarah that makes her different from the rest?" I asked him.

He replied immediately, "She makes me feel motivated. Like I can take on the world and win."

"What else?" I asked.

"Okay. Three words. She's smart, she's thoughtful," he paused a moment, "and she's classy."

"Classy?"

"Yes. She always dresses nicely, and she's got poise."

I got to meet Sarah a month or so later when Alan invited Wendy and me out on his sailboat. We anchored in a bay and while the others prepared lunch, Sarah and I had a chance to chat.

"You two really hit it off," I said.

"So far it's looking good."

I chuckled. "How come?"

"I think Alan's amazing. He has loads of things going, yet he always has time for fun, for living life—like with this boat and sailing."

"Is that what attracted you?"

"Well, I love that about him, but it wasn't the first thing, actually. The day I met him, after he helped me with my car, I insisted on buying him a coffee to thank him, and we ended up talking for over an hour about politics of all things, because there was an election going on at the time. And he really listened thoughtfully to what I had to say and asked good questions. And yes, he was good-looking and funny and all that, so you may not believe this, but I felt he took me seriously in a way other boyfriends hadn't. And that's what made me start to fall for him."

Alan fulfilled a certain need in Sarah—he made her feel bright, right, savvy, and whole—and for her part Sarah made Alan feel motivated, alert, and strong. They were the answer to each other's questions.

Know Yourself First

When most of us are asked what we're looking for in a potential mate, we usually describe some of their attributes: "someone with a great sense of humor," or "she'll have a lot of energy and a spirit of adventure," or even the classic "tall, dark, and handsome." But we'd be better off if we focused not on the person we're looking for but on ourselves—and in particular, on the way that ideal person would make us feel. As I said in the introduction, we don't actually fall in love with a person; we fall in love with the feelings we get when we are with them. That's what Alan and Sarah were getting at. They each enjoy the feelings they get when they're around each other—or, for that matter, when they even think about each other.

To figure out what it would take to make you feel complete, answer these two simple questions:

1. Do you consider yourself to be a more rational or more emotional person?

2. Would you describe yourself as socially outgoing or socially reserved?

Sarah answered *rational* and *socially reserved* to these questions, while Alan answered *rational* and *socially outgoing*. Peas in a pod on one side, they're opposites on another: matched opposites.

The table on page 45 will help you gain insight into your own personality and help you figure out what type would best complement you. There are no right or wrong answers, so just use your instincts. Start by eliminating the quadrants that definitely don't apply to you, then look at the remaining ones to see which is the best match to your personality. There may be one or two things in that quadrant that don't apply, but let them go. Not everything will be a perfect fit. And remember, this is what *you* think about yourself, not what other people think about you. Just be honest. No one else is going to read it.

Emotional

For centuries, thinkers have broken personalities down into these four main types. Hippocrates, the father of modern medicine, referred to them as *phlegmatic, choleric, melancholic, and sanguine,* after the human body fluids he believed influenced personality traits. Groundbreaking psychiatrist Carl Jung called his four types *thinkers, sensors, feelers,* and *intuitors.* Whatever the names, the categories are remarkably similar. Today, many professional organizations that deal in sales, education, and motivation use more or less the same breakdown. The DISC system, for example—*D* for dominance (controller), *I* for influence (promoter), *S* for steadiness (supporter), and *C* for compliance (analyst)—has been used to profile the personalities of more than 50 million people over the last 30 years, and the McCarthy 4MAT system is widely used all over the world to teach how individuals, groups, and organizations learn and respond to information. Although these profiling systems vary somewhat and use different labels, the four personality types they identify are very similar.

MORE RATIONAL THAN EMOTIONAL

1 Analyst
- Perfectionist
- Neat and organized
- Detail oriented
- Conscientious and correct
- Systematic and accurate
- Likes to plan ahead
- Follows directions precisely
- Likes facts and logic
- Intolerant of carelessness
- Dislikes unpredictability

Responds well to being right
Reacts badly to being wrong
Key Feeling: *Intelligent*

2 Controller
- Enterprising
- Quick and decisive
- Direct and self-assured
- Action oriented
- Likes power and prestige
- Restless
- Has large ego
- Strong-willed and strong-minded
- Can be argumentative
- Dislikes indecision

Responds well to getting results
Reacts badly to losing control
Key Feeling: *Powerful*

3 Supporter
- Reliable and a good listener
- Sympathetic and cooperative
- Enjoys working behind the scenes
- Loyal, sincere, and supportive
- Feels deeply, but hides emotions
- Modest, unassuming, and patient
- Cares deeply for people
- Does not like sudden changes
- Honest and reliable
- Dislikes insensitivity

Responds well to acceptance
Reacts badly to rejection
Key Feeling: *Valued*

4 Promoter
- Enthusiastic
- Persuasive and entertaining
- Spontaneous and friendly
- Loves to share ideas
- Expressive talker
- Enjoys recognition and prestige
- Dislikes filling in forms
- Can be disorganized
- Prefers face-to-face contact
- Impatient
- Dislikes routine

Responds well to admiration
Reacts badly to disapproval
Key Feeling: *Important*

SOCIALLY MORE RESERVED · **SOCIALLY MORE OUTGOING**

MORE EMOTIONAL THAN RATIONAL

In general terms, each personality type has a key feeling that needs to be validated. Analysts need to feel intelligent, controllers like to feel powerful, promoters do best when they feel important, and supporters like to feel valued. And in talking with people in long-term, vibrant relationships about how their matched opposites completed them, it was these feelings that came up again and again. "I feel like the cleverest guy in the world when I'm with her," an analyst would tell me. A controller might say, "He makes me feel strong." And a supporter would tell me, "She makes me feel needed." What's more, when asked about previous relationships that hadn't worked out, people readily saw the lack of these key feelings as the cause.

The Language of Love

When asked, "How does the one you love make you feel?" obviously not everybody used the words intelligent, powerful, valued, or important. But the vast majority of respondents did convey these feelings in various ways. Some of the words they used are in the table on page 48. It boils down to the need to feel intelligent, to feel powerful, to feel valued, and to feel important. Sure, most of us need to feel all of these things or combinations of them at one time or another, but socially, one always overrides the rest. Analysts are rational thinkers and socially reserved. They are more interested in getting things right than in getting who will complete you?

them done. They make rational, logical decisions, abhor being wrong, and in public need to be thought of as intelligent. Controllers are rational thinkers and socially outgoing, and they're happiest when they feel powerful. They get things done, but they've probably been called "bossy" or "controlling" at some point in their lives. Controllers need to be thought of publicly as powerful.

Someone who is an emotional thinker and socially reserved is likely a supporter. He or she likes to be valued by others for his or her caring, support, and reliability. Someone who's an emotional thinker and socially outgoing, on the other hand, is likely a promoter, a persuasive social butterfly who loves to be the center of attention. It's important for him or her to feel important.

Given that they're matched in the ways that are important to them (interests, values, religion, etc.), people who belong in opposing quadrants have a better chance of forming a lasting bond than people who fit into the same quadrant. Imagine two power-seekers rowing the same boat, both jockeying for the dominant position, both wanting to set the course, pace, and rhythm. Imagine how far two importance-seekers will get as they vie for attention. Or how about two intelligence-seekers setting off on their cruise, criticizing each other's decisions and putting each other down so they'll feel smarter (or, conversely, living in constant fear that they'll appear stupid compared to their mate). Or how

Intelligent	Powerful	Valued	Important
Sensible	Courageous	Safe and secure	Like a hero
Clever	Confident	Cherished	A highflier
Shrewd	Motivated	Indispensable	Famous
Correct	Strong	Useful	Persuasive
Insightful	Like a champion	Part of something	Expressive
Wise	Self-propelled	Lovable	Popular
Taken seriously		Peaceful	Influential
Perfect		Precious	Optimistic
		Interesting	

about two value-seekers looking to each other for support and just rowing along, preferring to agree to anything the other says and procrastinate, rather than rock the boat.

Better to pair a promoter with an analyst and have a fun-filled and well-planned trip, with one partner willingly embracing the other's need to feel smart. Or pair a controller with a supporter and have a confident captain and a willing crew. Or put a supporter with a promoter and have a floating fun palace. You get the idea. One plus one still equals two, but when those two are matched opposites, the possibilities seem infinite.

If you've already stepped on your partner's key feelings, use your understanding of what makes him or her tick to repair the situation. Reassure your analyst that she's intelligent and you respect her ideas, make sure your supporter feels valued, and so on. And in the future, be sure to treat your partner's key feelings with care.

The Second Time Around

I've known Michael since he was a fourteen-year-old schoolboy and have seen him sporadically over the years. Today he is the CEO of a textile company with more than 450 employees. Michael and I were having lunch one day when his friend Brian dropped by our table to say hello. We invited him to join us, and during the course of the conversation I learned that Brian is happily married to Virginia, Michael's ex-wife. What's more, Brian and Virginia have custody of Michael's children. Michael has been happily remarried for 12 years to a woman named Kim.

The two guys have a terrific attitude about the situation and were happy to discuss it with me. I began by asking them how they felt about the statement I introduced earlier: We don't fall in love with other people; we fall in love with the feelings we get when we are with them. They both agreed it made sense.

I then asked Michael to complete this sentence: "More than anything, Kim makes me feel _____." "That's easy," he replied, "unstoppable." I asked him, "Did Virginia ever made you feel unstoppable?" He chuckled. "No way."

Try It for Yourself

Put these findings to the test. Let's say you are a promoter and are supposed to feel most alive with someone who makes you feel important. Look back over your life and relationships with other people—and not just people you've been involved with romantically but also friends, coworkers, etc. Were the people with whom you felt at your best also the ones who made you feel important?

I asked Brian to answer the same question regarding Virginia. It didn't take him long to say, "The word that comes to mind is 'sensible.'"

I followed up by asking Michael if Virginia ever made him feel sensible. "Actually, she made me feel a bit insecure, if you must know."

At the time, I was putting the finishing touches on the self-assessments at the end of this chapter and asked Michael and Brian to have a go at them right there in the restaurant, over dessert and coffee. Michael was first to finish: "Nothing to it." He shoved his results over for me to see. As I suspected, he is a controller. Brian took a lot longer and quibbled with me about details and about it not being perfect. Michael laughed and leaned toward him, saying, "I've got you figured: You're an analyst." Brian laughed, "Yeah, you're probably right."

I asked whether they'd mind if Virginia and Kim filled in the assessment too—without their interfering. A few days later they e-mailed me the results. Virginia is a controller and Kim is a supporter.

All four of these people are matched socially, culturally, intellectually, and even physically, but Virginia and Michael's marriage hadn't worked out because they are both controllers. Virginia's second marriage, to Brian, and Michael's, to Kim, are successful because they've both found their complementary psychological opposites.

Mutual Enthusiasm

Many relationships begin solely as a result of exterior perceptions: We see someone who looks good to us and we try to build from there. But as in any other kind of construction, you need a solid, balanced foundation to make it last. As you go through this chapter and complete the self-assessment survey below, you'll discover what kind of person you are, what feelings make you come alive in love, and what kind of person is most likely to be your matched opposite. But love is all about mutual enthusiasm: Things just click when you are with the right person, and they double click when it's happening for both of you. In the end, the goal is to free you from trying to make things work, from trying to shoehorn yourself into incompatible relationships, and to find a match who completes you as much as you complete him or her.

Mental Minefields

The quickest way to blast a hole in a relationship (especially if it turns out you aren't matched opposites) and to bring out the worst in your partner is to trample on his or her key feelings. These feelings drive their behavior and sense of self, and over time, damaging them can have serious consequences.

For example, controllers thrive when they feel they are keeping things in line and that all systems are working smoothly. Avoid making your controller feel as if he is losing control or he could become a bully. You could eventually drive him to look elsewhere to reestablish his sense of power.

Good relationships come easily. Start to notice what kind of people you're most comfortable with. I can't tell you how many times people have said, "What I like about so-and-so is that I don't have to work at it." It's a terrific clue to a good relationship. Be on the lookout for people with whom the talk and the connecting come easily. If things don't click for both of you, don't blame or criticize yourself for failing. Be gracious if you are the one to decide it isn't working for you, then move on. If the other person is the one to say, "You're great, but I don't think you're the one for me," believe

Likewise, if you habitually embarrass or humiliate your analyst, she may become a nag or a complainer and there may be no returning to how things were. In the long term, you run the risk that she will leave and look for respect from someone else.

You can do many things to your promoter, but if you ignore or disapprove of him too many times, he will explode and then sulk. He may be forced to go looking for appreciation and importance elsewhere.

A supporter will put up with a lot, but if you constantly reject her feelings, she'll curl up in a ball inside and take a very long time—if ever—to trust you again. Eventually she'll go off in search of understanding, value, and acceptance in someone else's arms.

them—and let go. Trying to change yourself into what you think that person wants won't work. You just can't force love.

Finding out who you are and what you need in a partner puts you in the right frame of mind to find your matched opposite, but being informed and willing is only half the game. Pretty soon you're going to have to socialize—to get out there and have some fun. If it doesn't come easily to you, I'm going to help you with that. I'll help you figure out where to look and how to connect. And frankly, as home-work goes, I'd say this is about as good as it gets!

Self-Assessment Exercises

The key to finding your matched opposite lies in knowing what makes you tick and what it takes to make you feel complete. These quick self-assessments can help you can gain that understanding.

What Kind of Person Am I, Part 1

Quickly read each statement and complete it with the phrase that best describes you. Have fun with this and go with your first thoughts, since they're probably the most accurate.

1. You are having a problem with your neighbor. You:

   A. Systematically consider each part of the problem and analyze potential solutions before you meet with the neighbor.

   B. Quickly come to a decision about how to solve it and then confront your neighbor.

   C. Talk with friends about the problem first and then talk with your neighbor to get his side of the story.

   D. Catch your neighbor when you see him outside and make a joke about what's been bothering you. Then, tell him in an offhand way how you might solve the problem.

2. You get a new job and need to move. When looking for a home to buy, you:

A. Do your own research via the Internet and the local newspaper. You determine the monthly payment you can afford before you go out with a realtor. You see a lot of homes and, before making an offer on one, you research the neighborhood carefully.

B. Contact a realtor and look at properties a couple times a week until you find one you like. If you get satisfactory answers to all your questions, you make an offer on the spot.

C. Look at houses until you find one you like. It takes a few months but your patience pays off. Before making an offer, take a close friend or family member to see the home a second or third time.

D. Ask around to find out where the "happening" areas are. Seek a realtor you can connect with, since you're going to be together a lot. Tell the realtor you only want to look in the "hot" areas.

3. You most enjoy being:
A. Right
B. In control
C. Accepted
D. Admired

4. Above all you try to avoid:
   A. Being embarrassed   C. Rejection
   B. Losing control   D. Being ignored

5. You feel best when you're around someone who supports:
   A. Your thoughts   C. Your feelings
   B. Your goals   D. Your ideas

6. You would describe the way you dress as:
   A. Conservative   C. Casual
   B. Functional   D. Stylish

7. You most dislike:
   A. Unpredictability   C. Insensitivity
   B. Indecision   D. Routine

8. When you make decisions they are generally:
   A. Planned   C. Carefully considered
   B. Decisive   D. Spontaneous

9. The word that best describes you is:
   A. Perfect   C. Reliable
   B. Enterprising   D. Enthusiastic

EXERCISE

10. You feel best when you're with someone who makes you feel:

A. Intelligent   C. Valued
B. Powerful   D. Important

What Kind of Person Am I, Part 2

Check all that apply. In a romantic relationship, you feel best about yourself and your relationship when your partner makes you feel:

A	B	C	D
❑ Sensible	❑ Courageous	❑ Safe and secure	❑ Impulsive
❑ Clever	❑ Confident	❑ Cherished	❑ Famous
❑ Shrewd	❑ Motivated	❑ Indispensable	❑ Persuasive
❑ Correct	❑ Strong	❑ Useful	❑ Expressive
❑ Insightful	❑ Like a champion	❑ Part of something	❑ Spirited
❑ Wise	❑ Self-propelled	❑ Steady	❑ Popular
❑ Like you're taken seriously	❑ Like a highflier	❑ Lovable	❑ Influential
❑ Perfect		❑ Peaceful	❑ Optimistic

Self-Assessment Scoring

Count up the number of times you answered A, B, C, and D in Part 1, then the number of words you circled from columns A, B, C, and D in Part 2. Add them together and record the totals on the next page.

A_____   B _____   C _____   D _____

If you answered mostly:

A. You are rational, task oriented, introspective, and socially less outgoing—an analyst.

B. You are rational, task oriented, and more socially outgoing—a controller.

C. You are emotional, people oriented, introspective, and socially less outgoing—a supporter.

D. You are emotional, people oriented, and socially more outgoing—a promoter.

What Kind of Person Will Complete Me?

Your personality type provides insight about your key needs and matched opposite.

Analyst	Controller	Supporter	Promoter
Needs to feel intelligent*	Needs to feel powerful*	Needs to feel valued*	Needs to feel important*

*Or any variations from the A, B, C, and D columns on page 57.

Look for someone who is a different personality type from yours, who matches you in many ways—values, outlook, goals—but who will complement your temperament and will validate your emotional needs.

getting out there

lready I can hear you thinking, "Okay, fine, I understand the theory, but how do I find this person who completes me and whom I complete? Even if I knew exactly what I wanted, it's not as though I can order them from a catalog."

True enough—there's no shortcut to locating your soul mate. I can help you make your matched opposite fall in love with you quickly, but you have to meet him or her before the magic can work. You've got to get out there. I know this advice is as old as the hills, but like any selection process, love is a numbers game: The more people you meet, the more chance you have of finding one who's right for you in the long term.

Of course, you have the right to remain silent and do nothing, but it won't get you very far. There's a well-worn adage in business that goes, "No calls, no interest, no sales." And sooner or later you end up with no money and no job! The same thing applies to the search for love. You have to take action, and I'm not talking about grabbing a drink with your best friends or popping into a club occasionally;

I mean making a concerted effort to mingle with people whose interests, values, and beliefs match yours. If getting out there doesn't come easily to you, or if what you've been doing hasn't brought the results you want, perhaps it's time to create a socializing action plan that will bring more activity, variety, and new people into your life.

The Art of Socializing

Our culture spends half its time leaving messages, talking on cell phones, staring at screens of one sort or another, or sitting behind the wheel of a car. Our great-grandparents didn't live this way; they had face-to-face conversations, told stories, eavesdropped, gossiped, wrote letters, and even went walking just for fun, not exercise. Our society is forgetting the art of socializing. We've come to believe that we live to work rather than work to live, and we no longer set aside time to meet new people.

This is a real shame because the human race has evolved in large part from our drive to seek out the company of others and share our experiences and adventures. It's how we make sense of our world and add spice to our lives—raving about a new restaurant, telling tales of our youth or the day before yesterday, discussing politics and the arts, or mulling over current affairs. Over the years socializing has changed, in large part thanks to advances in science and technology. Once upon a time we congregated face-to-face in pubs, clubs, and churches, at festivals or outings, and by inviting people into our homes. More and more though, this face-to-face contact has been supplanted by leaving, retrieving, and responding to messages.

The only way to bring vitality back into our lives is by going out and interacting with other people. So, over the next few weeks, I want you to focus on improving your social skills and cultivating friendships both new and old.

Get Social

The best way to begin to meet new people is through the people you already know—your friends, family, and colleagues. Again, I realize this is not earth-shattering knowledge, but sometimes the obvious bears repeating. Starting close to home ups your chances of meeting people who share your social values. Let your friends know you want to meet people. Sure, you think they already know, but have you told them outright? If not, make sure you do.

This is a time in your life to make socializing a priority, turn it into a habit, and get good at it. Agree to set aside just one day a week for the next year to get involved with the people you already know, those you only know vaguely, and some you have yet to meet. Ask an acquaintance out for coffee or entertain friends at home. Join a community club or a volunteer organization. Invite friends to a sporting event, park, museum, concert, or festival, and suggest they bring friends too. The number of people you know will increase dramatically, along with your pool of potential partners. You'll probably even have fun while you're at it. Make some plans right now, and then follow through with them. You'll be surprised at the results.

Two Simple Rules

George lost his wife Nancy to illness when he was 55. They'd been best friends, and although they'd also had a few other close friends, they spent much of their time together. As the months went by after Nancy's passing, George became quite lonely. Then he attended one of my talks and heard me give my two simple rules for meeting people: Entertain once a week without fail, and accept all invitations.

George contacted me through a friend and told me this story: "The same night I heard you talk, I bumped into a young woman I'd met a couple of times. Her name's Michelle; she's the daughter of one of Nancy's friends. She inquired how I was doing, then told me she was helping to put on a weekend jazz festival and asked if I'd like to attend. She told me Main Street would be closed off, and there'd be lots of people there of all ages, and if I turned up she and her husband would look out for me. I thanked her. I was truly moved, but no way was I going to go. She was probably half my age and it just seemed too odd. Then, on the way home,

I started thinking about what you'd said, and the first thing that came into my head was the bit about entertaining and accepting all invitations. I had this flash; it seemed so obvious. 'Why not?' I thought. 'I just got an invitation.' That's when it all began."

Over the next few days George called a couple of friends and invited them to join him, and that weekend they all met up and went to the festival. "I actually enjoyed myself. We bumped into Michelle and her husband, Rick. It was a warm night, the music was pretty good, and heck, there's a world out there."

George made up his mind to entertain once a week no matter what, at first inviting friends, family, and colleagues, and encouraging them to bring a friend or two—the more the merrier. At first he was a bit concerned because he was a truly terrible cook, but as he told me later, this turned out to be the best thing he had going for him. "Word got out," he laughed. "So, when I'd invite people over for dinner, they'd ask if they could help—which meant the party started in my kitchen and just got better from there. Or people would ask me to come over to their place instead. So I'd end up meeting all their friends."

> Two simple rules for meeting people: Entertain once a week without fail, and accept all invitations.

George stuck to the advice he'd heard in my lecture—both parts. He accepted all invitations within reason—but reason included quilting exhibitions as well as golf tournaments— and entertained once a week. A little more than two years after Nancy passed away, George remarried. "I definitely never set out with this in mind," he stressed. "It's just that I got to know so many people that my whole life changed."

Maryanne, in her early twenties, is another case in point. I'll never forget the first words she spoke when she introduced herself at one of my workshops several years ago: "I'm so used to jerks I can't even recognize the nice guys anymore." Ever since childhood, Maryanne explained, she had been uncomfortable being on her own. "I'd cling on to just about anyone for company rather than be alone. I've had my share of heartbreak."

She shared a house with three other people, a guitarist who was away on tour most of the time, the guitarist's girl- friend, and a young philosophy student who was in year two of an affair with a married professor. They all had their sep- arate spaces in the house, but nevertheless it wasn't the sort of environment that lent itself to leisurely entertaining.

Perhaps because of her fear of being alone, Maryanne embraced the idea of creating a socializing action plan. It took some creative thinking at first, because she had to find a way to do it so that it didn't depend too heavily on bringing people over to her place, but before long she had become a sort of social facilitator. "One day I might phone some friends or acquaintances and suggest we go to a movie," she explained. "I'd pick up the tickets ahead of time so we could meet and have a coffee before the movie." Another day she'd phone a different group and suggest they meet up at an art opening or local fair. Yet another day she'd pull together a group to go bowling, or to hear an author speak at a bookstore. She ended up knowing dozens and dozens of people and had no trouble getting dates. As she got a better grasp of the principle of completion (see chapter 2) she learned to reject the jerks and focus in on the good guys, and after a while she met and married her Prince Charming. Today Maryanne is the wife of a diplomat in the Foreign Service—and entertaining in style.

So here you have it, two simple rules:

1. Arrange dinner or an outing once a week, and encourage your guests to bring new people.

2. Accept all reasonable invitations.

It doesn't have to be elaborate: "Hey, I'm having some friends over for potluck on Friday night. Why don't you come and bring a friend? I want to meet new people." Or, "There's a gang of us going to the movies on Tuesday. Want to come along? And feel free to bring a friend; I want to meet new people." There's the key phrase: *I want to meet new people.*

Get Involved

If you don't naturally meet a lot of new people, and you feel you've tapped your friends enough, find other ways to get involved. The more activities you participate in and the more places you visit, the sooner you'll get to meet the person who's out there searching for you. Take courses, volunteer, join a committee, go to exhibitions, walk someone's dog, learn to cook, take tango lessons, visit art galleries, go to pet shows, take up roller-skating, attend weddings and christenings, funerals, and other events.

Don't stop there. Get a fun part-time job, give dinner parties, start a book club, attend night school, ride a horse, take banjo lessons, study Chinese, learn spot welding. Not only will these activities make you a more interesting, vital person, but they'll also enlarge your circle of acquaintances.

Internet Dating

In 1727, Helen Morrison, a lonely spinster in Manchester, England, placed the first lonely hearts personal, advertising for a husband in the local weekly newspaper. In response, the town mayor committed her to a lunatic asylum for a month. But in hindsight, Helen Morrison was a pioneer.

Exactly 240 years later, and just a few miles away, the Beatles recorded *Sgt. Pepper's Lonely Hearts Club Band.*

One year earlier, their "Eleanor Rigby" ("All the lonely people/Where do they all come from?") had half the world humming to Helen Morrison's dilemma. The Beatles were pioneers too.

Flash forward thirty years and the explosion of online dating services has created a new way for lonely hearts to wait at the window, looking for true love. It sounds pathetic when you phrase it like that, but people sitting alone in front of their computer screens is only one side of the coin. On the other, I've heard about many happy couples who met online. And there's the crux of the matter: They met online, *then* they met in the real world, and then they fell in love. The Internet was a tool they used for meeting people—just as getting an introduction from a friend, joining a club, or taking classes is a tool. It helped facilitate their meeting in person, where they could truly learn about each other, face-to-face.

> Think of the Internet not as a substitute for socializing but as one of many ways you can expand your circle of acquaintances.

More than 40 million Americans log on to Internet dating sites every month, but the one thing I don't want you to do is sign up for a service instead of exploring other methods. Rather, think of the Internet as one slice of a larger pie—not as a substitute for socializing, but as one of many ways you can expand your circle of acquaintances, get together with them in a social setting, and eventually find your matched opposite.

Online daters tend to fall into three main categories, with umpteen variations. I call them the *realists*, the *romantics*, and the *disappearing acts*. The realists use online dating as an introduction service, to do some selecting and rejecting. When they find someone who looks interesting they set up a casual date to see if there's any real chemistry. The process is easier than going to a party hoping to meet someone—you're not emotionally invested at the outset, just interested; it's healthy and realistic; and there's always the possibility it will lead to love.

Then there are the romantics, who go and fall in love before they ever meet. Studies show that e-mail relationships can get far more intimate far faster than the real thing. People get seduced by the e-mail back-and-forth and start fanning the flames of emotional intimacy before there's any kindling, any spark, or even a twinkle in the eye. Some might pick up the phone to talk (a big deal for some), but often the e-mail conversation will go on for weeks without even that—and then they come face-to-face, with a lot on the line. Maybe there's a real spark, maybe there isn't, but chances are they've put the cart before the horse. Often there's been so much buildup that the actual meeting is a letdown.

In the third category are the disappearing acts, as they're called in the business. These are the ones who instigate a connection, lead you on, and then suddenly disappear. Of course, this happens in real-life dating too, and it can be almost as much of a letdown online.

Internet dating is here to stay and it's only going to grow, but it's still just a way to meet people, another option. And no matter how finely tuned the selection process and how optimistic the players, it still comes down to those first 90 seconds when you meet for the first time and make your initial impression, and those first 90 minutes when you start to really learn about each other. Here are some thoughts to take into consideration. First we'll run through the advantages and disadvantages, then I'll suggest some maxims for making your search more productive.

Advantages

There's no question that everyone on the site is looking to meet someone. So, there's none of the awkwardness and uncertainty you have in some social situations, where a person's relationship status or even sexual orientation may not be obvious.

- By reading people's profiles closely, you can quickly weed out people whose interests, age, values, religion, or whatever else don't appeal to you. Ditto when posting your own profile: Describing yourself honestly and being clear about your values and interests makes it more likely that someone compatible will write to you.

- Typically, a photo or even multiple photos will accompany a person's profile. The eyes truly are the windows of the soul, and being able to pair a face with the words in the profile definitely helps give you a clearer idea of the person you're writing to.

- The initial anonymity of the Net empowers shy people to approach people and make moves that they never would in person.

- You can meet people you wouldn't otherwise meet because your social and/or business circles don't intersect, or because you don't frequent the same places.

Disadvantages

- You can get hung up on Internet flirting: It's addictive and it's easy, and it's a short-term remedy for loneliness or boredom. But it's essentially blind: Our instincts about a person are based not just on what ideas they want to communicate, but on appearance, body language, facial expressions, and tone of voice—all subtleties that are lost when communicating via computer, no matter how many emoticons you use. Unless you get beyond the e-mail stage, the Internet will do you no good at all.

- Internet dating is limiting in the sense that you'll only be meeting folks who spend time on the Internet, which excludes a whole raft of people, especially if you're in the over-40 age bracket.

Advice

Here are a few good rules that should help those just getting their feet wet with Internet dating and also those who may have been using a service but haven't gotten the kind of results they'd hoped for.

- *All Internet dating sites are not created equal.* Just like bars or clubs, different sites tend to attract different types of people, but that isn't often obvious until you've read a number of profiles. Some of the larger sites, like Match.com, Yahoo! Personals, Date.com, MatchMaker.com, Udate.com, and AmericanSingles.com cater to a broad, mainstream audience. Others, like Lavalife.com and the personals on Salon.com and TheOnion.com, attract edgier, more urban and artistic singles. Some sites, like Nerve.com are more tilted toward sex than relationships. Other sites cater to specific constituencies: PlanetOut.com is for gays and lesbians; ThirdAgePersonals.com is devoted to aging baby boomers and active seniors; SeniorFriendFinder.com is more focused on older seniors. AsiaFriendFinder.com, BlackPlanetLove.com, and Jdate.com (catering to Jewish singles) provide opportunities for meeting people in your particular ethnic/cultural community, while eHarmony.com and Tickle.com concentrate on matching by personality.

And this is just for starters. Check out a variety of sites so you can see which feels most in keeping with your interests, lifestyle, and life stage, and attracts a clientele that's in line with your personality type and your values. After a while, if you aren't meeting people you like, try a different site.

- *Make sure your profile serves you well.* You want your profile to reflect your best self, so invest the time to make it well written and lively. Also take the time to get a good photo of yourself. A survey commissioned by ThirdAgePersonals.com asked, "When looking at someone's online profile, what makes you want to contact them?" Men rated a great smile, a good sense of humor, and a good figure/physique as the top three turn-ons. For women, a good sense of humor and similar taste in music, movies, books, etc. took the top two spots, with strong family values and a great smile sharing third place. When it came to turn-offs, both men and women listed people looking to cheat, negative attitudes, couch potatoes, and poor spelling or grammar as the worst offenses. And regarding the photo, the survey found that weight matters more to men than women; tacky clothes and a bad haircut matter more to women than men.

- *Be honest when creating your own profile, and keep your radar up when reading others'.* Many, many people have told me that when they finally meet someone they've been writing to, they find that person misrepresented him- or herself. Men seem to be the greater culprits in this regard. One woman I spoke with spent several weeks e-mailing with a man who claimed to be 40, but when they finally met he was closer to 60. His explanation? "Younger women didn't write to me when I put my real age." Well, duh! When reading others' profiles (and their e-mails, if you start to correspond), imagine you're reading their résumé. Does anything read strangely? Any mysterious gaps? Does anything just give you a funny feeling about the person? As for creating your own profile, resist the urge to punch up your image. Instead, just say who you are and what you're looking for in life. After all, you want someone who'll be attracted to *you,* not to some mythical person you've invented.

• *Save yourself from your own imagination: Make a date as soon as you decide you might like someone.* Often, people will e-mail for weeks before one of them suggests a face-to-face meeting, and during that time they can build up mental images of each other that bear no resemblance to the real people. As I said above, a person's appearance, body language, facial expressions, and tone of voice are the real primal elements of attraction, not whether your taste in movies and books match. So, when you meet someone online and feel a twinge of attraction, act. Ask the person for a drink or coffee, or to dinner if you've developed a par-ticularly good connection. Consider this part of the first

simple rule we discussed earlier: "Arrange dinner or an outing once a week." (Caveat: Because Internet dates are
essentially blind dates, but without common friends who
could vouch for the other person, it's wise to err on the side
of caution, especially if you're a woman. Arrange your first
encounter at a public place like a café, and don't accept a
lift home until you've gotten to know the person well.)

- *Don't fall into window-shopper syndrome.* When you do a
search and find 800 possible matches, it's very easy to start
collecting people in your favorites folder, then end up never
writing to any of them. Be bold: When you see someone
whom you think you'd like to meet, write to him or her
immediately. All it takes is a few sentences, because they'll
be able to read your online profile to get the bigger picture.
And remember, not everyone you write to will write back,
just as you probably won't respond to everyone who writes
to you. As in the real world, your odds of meeting people
improve the more you put yourself out there.
- *Practice discretion.* Don't reveal your full name, phone
number, or address in the early stages of a relationship.

Yes, But . . .

I know. I hear some of you protesting already: I have no
time, I'm not gregarious, I need to be pushed, there's no
one out there. What you're really saying is, "I'm better at
dreaming up excuses than I am at getting on with it." You'll

have to overcome your own mental obstacles, and here's how to do it, step by step.

1. "But I'm shy."

It's said that most people's biggest fear is public speaking—standing up in front of a group of fresh faces and delivering your ideas—and that this fear holds millions of people back from advancement in their careers. But if you ask people who've gotten past this fear for their secret, nine times out of ten they'll tell you all it took was practice. The same applies to connecting with fresh faces in your private life.

> Choose a class where you participate rather than sit back and listen to a lecturer.

Start small and safe and grow from there.

Take the initiative and begin with your close friends, family, or even colleagues at work. Ask them to introduce you to someone new. It doesn't have to be a potential mate, just someone who will lead you toward meeting more new people.

Socially reserved people frequently look at socially outgoing types and think, *Why can't I do that? Why can't I just walk up to a group of people and start talking?* I'll tell you why: Because it's not in your temperament. I'm socially outgoing, and my style is to flit from person to person and chat

(continued on page 78)

My Socializing Action Plan

Taking the Initiative

Take a moment to consider your favorite types of social activities:

❑ Dinners at home with close friends

❑ Parties

❑ Casual dining

❑ Fine dining

❑ Coffeehouses

❑ Sporting events

❑ Individual/pairs sports (golf, tennis, bowling, etc.)

❑ Team sports (softball, basketball, volleyball, etc.)

❑ Nature hikes/picnics/parks

❑ Music clubs (jazz, rock, R&B, etc.)

❑ Symphony/opera/ballet

❑ Theater

❑ Movies

❑ Outdoor festivals (cultural, music, flea markets, etc.)

❑ Dancing

❑ Nightclubs

❑ Sports bars

❑ Local bars/pubs

❑ Other: _____

Choose one activity from the list to create a social event around: _____

_____

Whom will you invite? _____

_____

_____

_____

Your date and time: _____

_____

_____

How will you invite them? (In person? By phone? By e-mail? By written invitation?) _____

_____

_____

On what day will you do the inviting? _____

_____

Are you going to ask your guests to bring friends? (Trick question: The only answer is *yes!*)

Photocopy your socializing action plan and stick copies on your bathroom mirror and on your refrigerator door.

(continued from page 75)

with them. My wife, Wendy, is initially socially reserved: Her style is to socialize with one person at a time. She's much happier spending an evening talking to two or three people in depth than moving from person to person at a big cocktail party. If you have learned to label yourself as shy, then my advice is to make friends one at a time—and change your self-label to something less limiting, like "cautious" or "reserved."

One way to meet people in a relaxed atmosphere is to take a course where people interact naturally. Choose a class where you participate rather than sit back and listen to a lecturer—something like cooking, wine tasting, or learning a foreign language should do the trick. You can also get involved in your community as a volunteer, which is an especially good method if you're new in town. Here's another place where the Internet comes in handy: Just type the name of your town or area, your state, and the word *volunteer* into a search engine, and see what comes up—it's almost guaranteed you'll find dozens of sites offering specific advice. Volunteermatch.org is one of the best, providing information on local volunteer opportunities throughout the United States.

2. "But I don't have time."

You have to make time. Sure you work ten hours a day and commute 45 minutes each way, but what do you want? Where are your priorities? Cheryl Richardson, author of

Life Makeover, recommends scheduling "breathing room" every day so you can step back, reevaluate your priorities, and be sure that you're working on what really matters. If you're reading this book, one of your priorities is meeting someone to love. Don't ignore this important part of your life! Set aside at least 15 minutes a day to phone or e-mail people and make plans. Call a friend on your cell phone on the way to lunch. Act on some aspect of your socializing action plan every single day, working toward your ultimate goal.

If you find it difficult at first to balance your action plan with other obligations or priorities in your life, find ways to combine the two. If, for example, exercising is a high priority for you, ask friends to join you on your exercise routine. Take a yoga class together, go swimming, or go for a walk or jog. If you have to go right home after work every day to take care of your dog, find a way to make this work for you. If you have friends or acquaintances with dogs, make dog play dates—and if you don't have friends with dogs, head for the local dog run and make some.

If you work long hours and aren't ready to scale back, try to have fun on your lunch break. If friends work nearby, meet them at a restaurant. If you work in a large office building, invite colleagues out for lunch and ask them to invite other colleagues—there's a good chance you won't know all of them. If you're flirting with someone through an Internet dating site and they work in the same geographical area, suggest meeting for lunch—it makes a great low-stress icebreaker. If you and your friends don't have the energy to cook for a potluck dinner after work, host a takeout potluck or order food to be delivered.

If your weekends are filled with house or apartment projects, arrange home improvement parties with friends in similar situations, with the host responsible for feeding his or her guest workers. Some of the projects might involve putting up wallpaper, painting a room, or cleaning out the attic—things no one likes to do alone anyway.

Time management solutions may not always be obvious, but if you're determined to find someone to love it's absolutely imperative that you make time to meet new people. If you find yourself still protesting, consider this: Maybe "I don't have time" is just an excuse. Maybe, when you get right down to it, you don't feel comfortable socializing, and your supposed lack of time is just a cover-up. Perhaps you're intimidated by people. Maybe you're short of money, and you're embarrassed by it. Maybe you think you're missing some basic etiquette skills: You're not sure which fork to use first and don't want to make a fool of yourself. If any of those sound familiar, just be honest with yourself, address the problem for what it is, and figure out a way around it. A simple Web search for *etiquette* and *silverware* will teach you the cutlery trick, and who knows, maybe your matched opposite doesn't know her salad fork from her dessert fork either—or maybe she'd be happy to teach you.

3. "But I live in a place so small that the phone book's one page long, and I already know everybody."

No matter how well you think you know a place and the people in it, there's always more to learn. Wendy and I live in a hamlet with a population of approximately 200, located five miles from a village with a population of about 2,000. Between the two there's a lot going on: church dinners, events at the library, dances, garden parties, Shakespeare nights, three country theater groups, at least two book clubs, a ski club, the annual fair, a yearly farm tour—and I could go on for a couple of pages. In fact, my first speaking engagement took place in the house of a young woman who organized a monthly film club. My daughter and I wandered into her little shop in the village and we struck up a conversation. I mentioned I was in the process of writing my first book, and she asked if I'd be interested in talking to her film club over snacks before the movie. I accepted, and duly spent 15 minutes discussing face-to-face communication. Talking to that tiny group in that small front room led directly to my putting on a small workshop, which led directly to my giving a seminar in a hotel ballroom, which led directly to my talking to 1,600 people at a national business convention a year and a half later. It's called networking, and most people these days know how it's done. You just have to learn that it works just as well in your private life as it does in your business life.

Circumstances are always changing, and people come and go, constantly presenting you with new opportunities for networking. But if you truly think you've exhausted all your resources, then spread your wings and look a little further away from home and your usual surroundings. Internet dating sites allow you to select the number of miles you're willing to travel to meet people. Instead of 10, pick 100, or even 500. Or, although it seems drastic, you could move—as Laura does in the next story.

4. "But I've just moved to town, and I don't know a soul."

You should consider yourself lucky—there are so many people to meet! So much potential! Again, take the initiative and get involved. Look at listings in the local paper, listen to the local radio station, talk to people in stores, or just drive around and look for places that seem interesting.

Let me tell you a story about a young woman I know.

A year ago Laura was working as an event planner in Boston, renting a one-room apartment for $900 a month and blowing $100 every day eating out and taking taxis. Her life was a constant hustle, and it seemed like every guy she met was obsessed with his work and didn't have time for her.

Laura decided to make a change. At 28, she quit her job, gave up her apartment, and headed for the small village of Two Elms, which she'd visited a couple of times and fallen in love with. There she rented a large, renovated, ground-floor apartment in an old country house beside a lake, less than five minutes' walk from the center of town. Her rent was less than half what she'd been paying in the city, and she could feed herself very nicely on less than $100 a week. Outside her window was a rambling garden, and the town itself was picture-perfect—the kind of place you see in the movies. But the move from Boston was a big leap of faith: Laura knew no one, and the job listings in the weekly paper rarely ran longer than an inch or two.

Laura was a private person by nature, but she consciously went out of her way to be friendly to everyone she met, greeting strangers with a smile and introducing herself to everyone behind the counter at the local shops. "Hi, I'm Laura," she'd say. "I just moved here." Her friendliness paid off. One month after she handed in the keys to her apartment in Boston, Laura began a part-time job at the Book Nook, a little bookstore squeezed between an upscale bakery and an antiques shop.

After working there for a few weeks, Laura secured a second part-time job selling wrought-iron flower boxes and light fixtures at the Ironworks, a storefront owned by an artist who did creative welding. Laura found her new work life fun and easy compared to her life in Boston, and it gave her time to do other things. She joined the theater restoration committee, and wrote a book review for the *Two Elms Times*. By the end of her second month, she'd made a few friends and gotten to know several of the regular customers at both stores, including Christina, an Austrian woman about twice Laura's age, who raised horses in the hills north of the village. Laura also had her eye on a young man named Jason who worked afternoons at the town pharmacy.

> Sit in the middle. That's where the popular people sit. That's where you get noticed.

As luck would have it, Christina tumbled into the Book Nook one Friday evening just as Laura was closing up, while at exactly the same moment Jason crossed the road and disappeared into the antique shop next door. The perceptive horsewoman caught Laura watching Jason through the glass and couldn't resist grinning at her new friend. "So, you like that young man, huh?"

"Ah, well, he is attractive. . . ." Laura was blushing.

"And what are you going to do about it?" asked Christina in her characteristically straightforward manner.

"I-I don't know," said Laura. "Nothing?"

Luckily for Laura, Christina wasn't just an expert at training horses; she was also quite a hand at roping in the fellas. "Come," she said, grabbing Laura by the arm, "let's go to the pub and discuss."

At the pub around the corner, Christina headed for the bar. "You find a table and I will get drinks—beer okay?" Laura nodded and went off to find a table in the far corner of the pub. Christina joined her minutes later carrying two sparkling pints, but she didn't put them down. Instead, she gestured to another empty table. "Over there; it's better." Laura grabbed her things and followed her friend to the table, which happened to be smack in the center of the room.

"You want to meet new people?" Christina said.

"Sure," Laura replied.

Christina leaned toward her. "Then you must always sit in the middle. That's where the popular people sit. That's where you get noticed. It is the same at horse shows. If you want the judges to notice you, place your horse in the middle. It is psychological. One year at school in Innsbruck where I grew up, they played this game with the seats in the classroom because they said the people who sit in the center are usually the most popular. They moved us around so everyone got a chance to sit in the center, and do you know what? At the end of the year everyone was popular. It's true. Now I tell all my riding students to head for the middle.

"Now, this young man," Christina continued. "Tell me about him."

Can a Woman Ask a Man Out?

Should a woman ask a man for a date? Conventional wisdom says, "No, it's the man's job to do the pursuing." Reality says, "Sure, why not?" And why not indeed? Because it works. I have met dozens and dozens of couples where the woman did the asking and the result is a happy, balanced, long-term life together.

What's the best way to do it? Ask without asking. Use an indirect or soft question. Did you ever notice that if you say to someone, "I wonder what time it is," they'll tell you the time, even though you didn't directly come right out and ask for the time. Or if you say, "I don't know what kind of movies you enjoy," they spill the beans and tell you. When you use a statement like this, especially with questioning body language—raised eyebrows or raised hands—and a questioning voice inflection, the person will willingly answer a question that was never even asked in the first place. This is a time-tested way for a woman to ask a man out on a date. It even works on paper.

"I can't," Laura answered. "I don't know anything but his name. I don't even know if he's available."

"He is. His boss boards his horses at my place and he never stops talking. "Now, have you ever spoken to him?"

Trina is a columnist with a large city newspaper. "I met James when we went for a business lunch—it was a Thursday," she told me one Sunday afternoon at a house party. "For two hours we talked about everything. I couldn't stop thinking about what a good time I had. I wanted to do something about it. On Friday I wrote a short thank you note that said, 'Thanks for a great lunch. I really enjoyed myself, and the conversation. I am not sure of your personal circumstances but, if you are able and would like to, I'd like to take you for dinner sometime.'

"Right after I sent the note I wanted to get it back but it was too late—it was gone. I went away for the weekend with some girlfriends, but I couldn't stop thinking about it. I was nervous, but didn't see that much downside, other than not hearing from him at all—which would have been equivalent to a 'no' and a little hurt to the ego.

"When Monday came, the phone rang and it was him. I felt relieved. We went for dinner on Tuesday night, and hey—now it's fifteen years later, and James still has the note."

"I had to ask him for advice at the pharmacy a few weeks ago when I had pinkeye." Laura laughed, sipping her beer and beginning to loosen up. "I looked gorgeous!"

"If you have been here for two months, then I think it is

time you give a dinner party," pronounced Christina, slapping her hand on the table. "And you are going to invite Jason."

"No, no, I can't." Laura put her glass down.

"Yes. You are going to find a way to talk to him and here is what you are going to say: 'I'm having a dinner party to celebrate being here for two months, and I'm inviting a bunch of people. I would love for you to come.' And here is what you call the kicker." Christina paused for effect. "Then say, 'Please feel free to bring a friend.' Then pause and add, 'if you wish.'"

"But I can't just walk right up to him."

(continued on page 90)

Getting Involved

A great way to meet people is to join a community group, a sports league, or a club or class devoted to an activity that interests you.

Step 1: What Are You Interested In?
❏ Sports leagues/clubs: golf, skiing, racquetball, basketball, bowling, etc.
❏ Pastime clubs: book, poetry, film, cards, bingo, stamp collecting, etc.
❏ Volunteer/outreach organizations

❑ Classes: dance, music, cooking, language, wine-
   tasting, woodworking, stained glass making, etc.
❑ Community recreation outings: hiking, cycling,
   scuba diving, fishing, etc.
❑ Religious clubs
❑ Political associations
❑ Other: _____

_____

Step 2: Name Something You've Always Wanted to Do/Learn

_____

_____

Step 3: Find Out How to Get Involved in That Thing
Look in your local newspaper and yellow pages, ask around, and search the Web for local organizations. Note the ones you find here:

_____

_____

_____

_____

_____

Step 4: On What Day Will You Make the First Move?

_____

(continued from page 88)

"Yes, you can. You see him, you count to three, and on three you go up and speak. Just like going over a steeple-chase jump. If you hesitate, you fail. You think about it, you fail. You feel afraid and your horse can tell, and it will shy away or just refuse. Same with men and women: You hesitate, you fail. Count one, two, three, and go. It's the *Three-Second Rule*. My students all know this rule. That way you are strong. You are not asking him out on a date, for heaven's sake; you are asking him to socialize—it is different and it is normal. Then you have him where you want him." She stopped and tapped her empty glass. "Another beer?"

Laura hesitated. Christina clicked her tongue as if to urge on a horse and Laura looked up.

"Oops! One, two, three," she said, counting off on her fingers, then answered confidently, "Yes, I'd love one."

Although the outcome of this story isn't the real point, of course you want to know what happened. Laura followed Christina's advice and invited Jason to her party, telling him to bring a friend if he wanted. He came alone, which suggested that he was interested in Laura. They dated for a while, but they didn't fully click. Laura, however, eventually found her matched opposite—Jason's cousin, whom she might never have met if she hadn't followed Christina's plan, three-second rule and all.

The real point of this story is to show you that regardless of circumstance you can always find ways to make connections.

And you can benefit from Christina's great advice. She showed Laura how to engineer a meeting with a man she was interested in, without it looking as if she were blatantly chasing him, something some guys still don't handle well. Rather than be pushy (which wasn't in her nature anyway), she simply set up a congenial situation where Jason could do the chasing if he was so inclined.

There Is No Rejection, Only Selection

One of the main reasons people are uncomfortable with dating and reaching out socially is the fear of rejection, but it's a mistake to look at it this way. As you search for your matched opposite, you are going to spend a fair bit of time dating, and because the search is a numbers game, you will likely experience what you may choose to label as rejection, as well as doing some so-called rejecting yourself. This is most apparent in online dating, where you might scroll through dozens of profiles before seeing any that interest you—and of course, the reverse applies as well. One of the major sites even has a counter showing how many people have viewed your profile since you last logged on. If you looked and saw that 130 people had read your posting but not a single one has been moved to contact you, you could think of it as a crushing rejection or simply realize that you probably weren't a good match for any of those people.

And as I said earlier, rejection isn't personal; it's part of the natural selection process. You wouldn't walk into a furniture store and buy the first sofa you saw. Instead, you'd start shopping with some general idea of what you want, then try out one after another until you found one that felt right. Most of the ones you'd reject would be perfectly fine sofas that would be great in someone else's living room—just not yours. You go through the same process of selection when buying a car, a house, and just about anything else of importance to your life, so it's absurd to think that you'd settle for the first man or woman that came along. Unless you're one of those extremely lucky souls who meets their matched opposite early, settling for someone you don't really click with would be downright foolish.

The fact is, most people you meet won't be your matched opposite—but they may make great friends. Or, as in the story about Laura and Jason, they may introduce you to your matched opposite. Be open to people's charms, but also be aware that very few of them would be a really great match for you. Likewise, you're not going to be right for everyone, either.

That Special Feeling

I'm sure there have been times in your life when you saw a piece of clothing or furniture in a store window and thought, "Wow! That's perfect for me." Can you recall how it felt? Maybe you've had a similar feeling when traveling, or when meeting people who later became your best friends. It's that blissful, relaxed feeling of just knowing you'll get along effortlessly, and probably be friends forever. Take a moment and remember how that felt.

On the opposite side of the coin, I'm sure you've met people who gave you a feeling of unease, though you might not have been able to say why. Given the choice, whom would you select to spend time with and whom would you reject? The first feeling is what you'll get when you click with your matched opposite—you'll just know he or she is right for you. It can't be forced or faked, and not just anyone can give it to you.

> **People who do the same thing over and over and expect different results are setting themselves up for disappointment.**

Go back and read these two paragraphs again slowly. Close your eyes and relive each feeling. Linger on what it feels like to just *know* something's right. Then you'll understand why rejection is a productive thing.

Welcome Rejection

Rejection is a course correction on your path to success, and instead of inspiring you to self-pity, it should inspire self-examination: "What did I learn?" you should ask yourself. And "What will I do differently next time?" If you don't welcome rejection you'll continue treading the same unconscious feedback loop: Make a move, get a response, react without thinking. Ask the wrong kind of person on a date, get rejected, feel rotten.

People who do the same thing over and over and expect different results are setting themselves up for disappointment. If you keep on approaching or falling for the wrong kind of guy or gal, it's not because you have some huge psychological problem or that there's something wrong with you; it's because you aren't stopping to process the feedback that each failure is providing. Look back on your old relationships and see if you can detect a pattern that you continually play out. Hopefully, you'll see where you go wrong, and you can use that information to recognize and understand the warning signals in the future. That's what Maryanne did when she finally figured out she'd been falling for jerks for so long that she'd forgotten how to recognize the good guys. Once she broke free of the loop, she found her career diplomat and lived happily ever after.

So as you go out and start meeting all these new people, what are you going to do when you get rejected? Handling rejection requires an immediate adjustment in attitude. If a person doesn't return your interest, that's not a cue to give up and get depressed, it's a call to move on! If you were an apple picker and you came upon a tree with no apples on its branches, would you take it personally and feel hurt and sorry for yourself? Of course not! You would just admit that there was nothing there for you and move on to the next tree. Feeling sorry for yourself means you've lost sight of your goal.

Most people will let you know they're not interested in a diplomatic way, but you'll probably meet some rude and ungracious characters along the way, too. When you do, just excuse yourself politely and give thanks that you found out what kind of person he or she was relatively quickly, before you got more deeply involved. Ideally, the rejection/selection process would be painless, but you'll probably get your feelings bruised once or twice. It's human nature to feel bad in situations like this—but don't. Instead, you have to welcome rejection/selection as part of the exploration, the journey, the adventure.

Understanding the principle that there's no rejection, only selection, means if you're on a date and things aren't clicking, it's not anybody's fault. It has nothing to do with you as an individual; it's not personal. It just means you and your date are not complementary psychological types. So, enjoy your time together, be yourself, remain polite and gracious. At the end say thanks and goodbye and move on to someone else—or remain friends, because friends will enlarge your social circle and enrich your life.

Everything Begins with You

Only you can make it happen. If you are not happy with the way things are going, you are the only one with both the authority and the responsibility to change them. You are in charge of your life—you say what gets done, and you reap the rewards.

One, two, three—no hesitation. This is the moment to take the initiative and get involved. Start slowly if that's your style but make socializing a priority in your life. By the end of a month you'll be an expert at mixing and mingling, and you'll wonder why the heck you didn't do this before.

PART 2
get set

———

Fine-tune your people skills so that

when you meet your matched

opposite, you are ready to connect.

a fabulous first impression

What makes a star a star? I don't just mean stars of stage or screen, but those people you see at a party or down at the garden center who attract and hold your attention longer than the average person—the ones you look at and somehow you want to be with them. What is it that attracts you to them? Is it the way they dress, the way they stand and move, or something ineffable they give off that creates this impression?

We've all heard the phrase "You never get a second chance to make a first impression," and it's true. People make judgments about you the moment they see you— and just because *you* haven't seen *them* doesn't mean they haven't noticed you. You don't have to be a star, but it won't hurt to have a little bit of star quality to help ensure that your first impression is working for you. That means you need to leave your house feeling good about yourself and the way you're dressed and to stay that way while you're in public. Because what people respond to when they see you for the first time, before you even open your mouth, are your attitude and your clothes.

A First Impression Begins with Attitude

Alicia, Dennis, and Naomi arrive at the same time to a gala fund-raiser at Boston's Copley Plaza Hotel. The organizers are expecting at least two dozen celebrities, 500 other guests, and the usual bevy of local media.

As the three enter the ballroom, their body language speaks volumes—three different volumes. Alicia is obviously there to enjoy herself. She's smiling, looking around, and walking tall. She appears natural and happy—she looks like fun. She scans the crowd, spots a friend, and makes her way purposefully toward her. Dennis, on the other hand, looks around skeptically, like he'd rather be anywhere else but here. He has his hands in his pockets, and if you had to guess what he's thinking, it would probably be, "What a load of bozos. How long before I can escape?" Naomi enters with a forced smile on her face but stops a few steps into the room. Her shoulders droop as she begins to psych herself out, and she looks like she's scanning for the closest corner to hide in.

Notice I kept using the word *looks*. That's what first impressions are based on: looks. And notice how their attitudes are apparent, too, when they enter the room. Dozens of people have seen them already, but only one, Alicia, has turned heads and made a good impression.

You can spot someone's attitude from half a block away, from the middle of a subway train, from the other side of a shop, or from the moment someone steps in the room. In my days as a fashion photographer we'd schedule one Friday a month for "go sees." This was when my staff and I, and sometimes my clients, would see 30 or 40 new models, male and female. Each one would get about five minutes to say a few words and show us their portfolio. In truth, though, we never needed five minutes. Five seconds was more like it. The moment a new face stepped into the room we knew whether or not the

> **You can spot someone's attitude from half a block away.**

person had what it takes. When we'd discuss the session among ourselves afterwards we didn't talk as much about individual features as we did about mood, or attitude. "Jane was peppy." "Mark looked kind of dramatic." "Dana looked dangerous." In that business—the business of first impressions—you can be the most gorgeous creature in the world, but if you don't have the right attitude, you don't have what it takes. And we could spot attitude in a flash—everybody can, and everybody does. Attitude is such a influential part of a first impression that my assistant made up a sign and hung it outside the studio door on go-see days. It read, "When you go through this door, it's your attitude more than anything else that'll make you or break you."

"Hi" and "Bye" Attitudes

There are two distinct classes of attitude—those that attract and those that repel. When you see someone who's happy, confident, and relaxed you're likely to be attracted to him or her. These are appealing "Hi!" attitudes. The opposite is true for someone who seems arrogant, gloomy, tense, angry, or dejected. No one wants to hang out with gloomy or irritated people because sooner or later they sap all your energy. They have "Bye" attitudes. The key to opening yourself up socially is to leave your gloomy side alone and consciously choose to look on the bright side— the side that gives you unlimited access to opportunity.

The good thing about attitude is you can adjust it whenever you want and buzz yourself up to the top of your game. All it takes is practice. Think about a time when you felt great. Perhaps it was when you accomplished something important to you—maybe you won a race or gave a great speech or scored a goal. Or it may simply have been a time when you were enjoying the company of friends or family, or the late afternoon light of a summer day, or when you just felt truly yourself. Whatever it was, relive it in your mind in as much detail as possible, and once it's so clear that you could almost reach out and touch it, connect it in your mind with a trigger word so you can summon that feeling again at will. Plenty of actors, TV personalities, and fashion models have trigger words or phrases to get them in the mood. Some will say "showtime" just as they head out into the spotlight and their whole being changes. They are "on"— they almost literally switch on a bright, energetic attitude. You can do the same. On page 108 in this chapter there's an exercise that will teach you to do this simply and easily.

Attitudes Are Contagious

Have you ever noticed when you're in a group, if someone tells a joke and one person starts genuinely laughing, the others start laughing too, even if the joke's not all that funny? The same happens with tension and sadness. That's because, as a species, we're hardwired to relate to the feelings and emotions that other people give off. This helps us adapt and fit into our environment. It works like this: If I smile at you, you'll feel inclined to reciprocate and smile back. In much the same way, if I look at you dismissively and then avert my eyes, you'll probably respond in kind. If I sigh, you feel it. If you laugh, I feel it.

Attitudes are contagious. They are, in fact, big bundles of feelings projected through body language, tone of voice, and the words you choose. When you're angry, you look angry, you sound angry, you use angry words—and it makes other people feel uncomfortable. Conversely, when you're

Thoughts and Emotions: The Chicken or the Egg?

What comes first, your thoughts or your emotions? The thought/emotion question is like the chicken and egg conundrum. One really doesn't come first; they're intertwined. Which means *thoughts affect emotions*. A whole area of psychotherapy, called cognitive therapy, is based on this simple principle and has been shown to be effective in dealing with depression, low self-esteem, eating disorders, and a host of other problems. So, change your thoughts (i.e., your attitudes) and you *can* change your feelings.

Many people have grown up believing that their attitude toward life is entirely a response to what happens to them. If it's raining and they were counting on sun, their attitude is annoyance. If their breakfast is cold, their attitude is

playful, you look playful, you sound playful, you use playful words—and it makes other people feel playful. Ditto for enthusiastic, or sexy, or any other mood.

This is the bad news and the good news all rolled into one. The bad part is that someone's miserable attitude can make everyone around them feel equally miserable. But, by the same token, a joyful attitude can make others feel joyful. You can make the most of this infectiousness, adjusting irritation. If a friend doesn't call when expected, their attitude is resentment—and so on. They believe that they are simply reacting to what comes their way.

But in fact, to a large degree you can *adopt* a positive outlook. As we go through our days and take in what's going on around us, we unconsciously talk to ourselves about what we see, hear, feel, smell, and taste. For some, this interior dialogue is empowering because they naturally look on the bright side. ("Ooh, look it's raining. That's great for the garden.") For others, it's gloomy self-sabotage ("It's raining. That sucks. It's going to be a lousy day.") But once you're aware of your self-talk, you can change the conversation. When you hear yourself saying something negative, refocus and try to find something positive—turn "Dammit, my shoes are getting wet" into "I love the sound of rain on the pavement."

your attitude to drive *others'* behavior. Be joyful and your upbeat mood will rub off on others.

How to Slip into an Attitude

Without the right attitude, you're not going to get very far in attracting your matched opposite, or anyone else for that matter. To achieve the results you want, you must think, walk, talk, and act in such a way that the best and

Actions Speak Louder Than Words

In face-to-face communication we first give credibility to what we see (to gestures and body language); then to the tone, pitch, and volume of voice; and, last of all, to the things that are said. There's solid scientific proof for this. In 1967, Dr. Albert Mehrabian, a professor at the University of California at Los Angeles, published a seminal study on face-to-face communication titled *Decoding of Inconsistent Communication* which showed that 55 percent of what we respond to is visual; 38 percent is auditory, or the pure *sound* of the communication; and only 7 percent involves the actual words we use. The main way we connect with others, as Dr. Mehrabian proved, is through physical gestures (posture, facial expression, movements) and rhythms (breathing speed, hand- or foot-tapping, nodding, etc.).

most attractive parts of your personality come out. Is your best nature funny and warm, sexy and confident, relaxed and reassuring? Make sure people know it. But remember, your body and mind are part of the same system and you can't hope to control one without the other. Sure, you can tell your face to smile, but it won't come off as genuine unless you first adopt the right attitude to put you in the mood.

So how do you go about adopting a "Hi!" attitude? It's not like a piece of clothing that you can just slip on and off at will, right? Actually, it is! In a moment I'll show you how to do it, but first I want you to answer these five questions.

1. Where is the milk in your refrigerator?

2. Is your favorite piece of music fast or slow paced?

3. What does sand feel like?

4. Does hot bread smell different from warm bread?

5. Do you prefer the taste of lemon or lime?

To answer these questions, you had to play back information that had been collected by your senses in the past and stored away. To locate the milk in your fridge, you made a mental picture and saw it there. To determine the pace of your music, you played part of it in your mind. You ran sand through your fingers, took imaginary sniffs of the bread, and had a quick mental taste of the lemon and lime.

Psychologists believe that our subconscious mind doesn't know the difference between something real and something vividly imagined—for example, imagine biting into a lime and you'll actually salivate. During the following exercise I'm going to ask you to make a picture in your mind. Don't expect to see Technicolor billboards right away. At first, your pictures will be as good as the one you made to locate the milk in your fridge.

Getting in the Mood

Choose one of the following attitudes: warm, playful, confident, or curious.

Say you chose confident. Now close your eyes and think of a *specific* moment in time when you felt the most confident you ever have—totally in control and knowing exactly what to do. Relive what you saw, heard, felt, and maybe even smelled and tasted at that moment, in as much detail as you can.

First, watch the scene unfold as if it were a movie. Look around and see what's going on in detail. Listen to all the different sounds. When you have the sights and sounds in focus, step into the picture. Instead of watching the movie, you're now in it. Notice the foreground, the middle ground, and the background. Make the colors bright and sharp and colorful. Bring up the sounds in detail—notice which direction they come from. Are they harsh or sweet? If there are smells and tastes, bring them in too, to make the most complete picture possible. Make it as real as you can.

Now attune yourself to the external physical sensations—the air temperature, the feel of your clothing, your feet, your glasses, your belt. Explore and relive whatever external sensations you can.

Now bring your attention to your internal feelings. Focus on your confidence. Notice where you feel it—in your tummy? Your shoulders? Your chest? Feel your posture. Are you standing tall? Is your head held high?

Take ownership of these feelings and pump them up. Make them bigger, stronger, brighter, and more intense—and then double them. Then double them again.

When you're bursting with the image, yell the word "Great!" in your mind three times. "Great, great, great!" Then again, "Great, great, great!" And a third time, "Great, great, great!"

When you are ready, open your eyes and savor the feeling. The exercise you have just done is a powerful one—but it's also very simple. You just relived, in detail, a time when you felt good, and now, when you say "Great!" three times to yourself, you can bring it whooshing back into the front of your mind anytime you like. Before you close your eyes and do the exercise again, make sure you memorize the four simple stages:

1. Play the movie.

2. Step in to see, hear, and feel it.

3. Pump up the sensations.

4. Yell "Great!" three times in your mind.

Standing Tall, Feeling Terrific

Research shows that the single most important attribute we all subconsciously seek in a potential mate is good health. This goes back to our earliest ancestors, and the desire to be fruitful and multiply: Females wanted clever hunters and strong protectors; males wanted mates able to bear healthy children. One way we determine health is by posture: Someone who's standing tall looks healthy and strong, ready to face the world. Your posture signals volumes about your physical and emotional health and vitality, and it does so in a flash.

Stand tall and you'll feel emotionally tall. Send the crown of your head to the sky, move your shoulder blades down and slightly back, and you'll feel on top of your game. Just as thoughts and emotions influence each other, so do body and mind. If you feel sad, chances are you'll be sitting slumped, with your head bowed and mouth turned down. If you feel happy, you'll be walking tall, head up and smiling.

But the reverse is also true: Physical attitudes influence moods! You can't feel happy while you sit in that slump with your mouth curled downwards (try it, it's true!) and you can't feel sad while you leap in the air with a big grin on your face. Your body just won't allow it. When you adjust your posture to upright and proud, your body will generate feelings of self-confidence, courage, and even sexiness. Let good posture enhance your desirability.

My Fabulous First Impression

What attitude or combination of attitudes would you like to exude when you meet someone new? Determining this is the first step toward achieving it. Finish the following sentences:

1. The me that I'd like everyone to see is _____.

2. The right attitude or combination of attitudes for me is _____.

3. To think, walk, talk, act, and conduct myself according to my selected attitude(s), I will use the following trigger memory: _____.

If you want to move on to some advanced poise and posture work, take dance lessons. Dancing benefits you in myriad ways. You gain strength, grace, and rhythm; it works wonders for your posture and gets you in touch with your body; and it helps boost your confidence, on the dance floor and off.

Here's Looking at You

So, you've got a great attitude, you're standing tall, you're just about ready now to go out and find your soul mate, right? There's only one thing we have to check before you head out the door: Just what is that you're wearing?

EXERCISE

Exercise: Poise, Pace, and Posture

Poise simply means to move with quiet confidence and grace. It is self-assuredness, not arrogance, and it's all about posture and pace. It's sexy and attractive, it turns heads and helps you control a room, and it all begins with excellent posture. Take a few minutes to go through this activity and then practice it regularly. Before you know it, poise will be a part of who you are.

It may seem corny, but modeling schools have an exercise that they've used for years, making both male and female students do it from day one. It's simple, and it works.

1. Put a dictionary on your head.

2. Walk around the room. It should take you about ten minutes to get used to the position and the balance of it.

3. Go in and out of doors, opening and closing them behind you.

4. With the book still balanced on your head, go up and down stairs.

5. Sit down, count to five, and stand up. Go to another chair and repeat.

6. During each stage, pause, close your eyes, and focus on your posture—on what it feels like, on how you're

holding your shoulders, your hips, your feet. Notice how calm your pace is and how graceful your overall carriage. 7. This is where you graduate: Drink a cup of tea or coffee with the dictionary still on your head, and promise yourself that from this moment on, whenever you see, drink, or think about tea or coffee, you'll imagine that big book of words is on your head and adjust your posture and pace accordingly.

Setting the dictionary aside, practice carrying yourself with grace and poise all the time—while you're walking the dog, while you're stuck in traffic, while you're waiting in line or watching TV.

If the first thing someone notices about you is your attitude, the second is your clothes. In fact, the impact is made so quickly it's as if they see both things at the same time, and then form their first impressions about you. Your clothing speaks volumes. It tells people what kind of person you see yourself as. It also can reveal a lot about your socioeconomic status, whether you're conventional or flamboyant, sexy or modest, trendy or traditional. Take a good hard look at your wardrobe and see if it makes the statement you want. Many of us are creatures of habit and we wear what we've always worn. But is the look you adopted 15 years ago (or more) still appropriate for you now?

Coco Chanel once said, "Dress poorly, and people will notice your clothes; dress well, and people will notice you." Ask yourself: What do I want my clothing to communicate to others? Is there an aspect of my personality that I want to emphasize? Does my current wardrobe do the job? Take into account your physical characteristics and make sure the image you want to create works with them.

Wearing attractive clothes with confidence makes you feel different about yourself and makes other people respond differently to you.

Get into the habit of looking your best when you go out. I'm not talking about always being perfectly coiffed and made up or wearing your fanciest duds. Rather, I mean you should dress so you feel attractive—so that if you ran into an old friend you hadn't seen for years, you'd feel that you looked fine. We're making first impressions all the time, and you never know whom you might meet.

Wearing attractive clothes with confidence makes you feel different about yourself and makes other people respond differently to you. The way we dress influences our behavior and attitude, and that in turn influences other people. The bottom line with clothes, as with other forms of packaging, is the better you dress, the more seriously people will treat you. That said, make sure that you're comfortable in your clothes, and that they convey the real you—at your best. If you adopt a look for the sake of fashion but it makes you feel uncomfortable, keep experimenting until you get to a look that feels right. Remember, people will sense your discomfort just as clearly as they see your clothes.

Also bear in mind that dressing well depends on the context of the situation and who it is you want to attract. If you're looking to impress the attractive woman with the designer sunglasses in the new Mercedes, chances are you're not going to do it in cutoff jeans and hiking boots. On the other hand, if you've fallen for a wilderness guide, then that ensemble might be just the ticket.

Seven Keys to Dressing Well

Clothes are far too personal an issue for me to give specific advice that would work for everyone. Instead, here are seven key points, based on what I learned in my years in the fashion industry, that will help make your clothes work for you. None of this is new: It's tried and true, and it works. Above all, remember the golden rule: Keep it clean and simple.

1. Wear Clothes That Fit

Many people wear clothes that don't fit correctly—they're a little too big, a little too small, not the right shape, a bit too short, a tad too long. But fit makes all the difference. The goal

Read the Signals

Just as your clothing speaks volumes about you, what others wear can give you insight into them. Learn to read the signals—beyond the instant assessments that we all naturally make. For example, different personality types feel more at home in certain types of clothing than others. You'll find dominant, controlling types lean toward a more tailored appearance; the analytical personality favors the formal, somewhat conservative look; the promoter goes in for the stylish and expressive approach; while the solid, supportive man or woman is more comfortable with the casual look.

is for your clothes to skim your body and hang well. Remember, size doesn't matter; fit matters. If you're not sure whether your clothes fit correctly, ask friends. If you're shopping, ask the sales help. A well-fitting, tailored jacket is the ultimate power garment for every wardrobe. Be honest with yourself. If you need help, ask a good tailor or dressmaker.

2. Accessories Make a Big Difference

The right accessory can make you look better dressed than you are. If you can't afford the most expensive and best quality when it comes to your wardrobe, splurge on accessories.

Buy the very best belt, shoes, purse, or scarf that you can afford. And remember, don't overdo it. Let one or two carefully chosen accessories make your statement. You want to avoid superficial distractions. The same goes for your jewelry—for men, a tasteful watch is all you need. For women, a simple necklace and carefully chosen earrings and you're set. If you want to wear more, just make sure that all your pieces are working together. In the end, you want to be remembered for your conversation, rather than for what you're wearing.

3. Make Sure Your Clothes Aren't Out of Date

The upside of following trends—that you look fresh, tuned in, and of the moment—is also its downside. When your clothes are out of date, you are out of date. So if you're going to wear up-to-the-minute fashion, stay abreast of the fads. Otherwise stick with more traditional fare. Or invest in some classics along with your "now" pieces so you don't have to replace your wardrobe every season.

4. Wear a Well-Coordinated Outfit

Make sure your clothes blend well together—and I don't mean simply avoiding pairing green and yellow stripes with pink and purple polka dots. Make sure your fabrics, colors, and styles all match; that they blend well together and are in the same family of casual or formal. And don't forget to factor in your accessories: A too casual belt or pair of shoes can throw off an otherwise perfect outfit. The idea is to attract, not distract. If you're in doubt about your look, ask for help. You'll get it for free at any decent clothing store.

5. Dress for the Occasion

If you have trouble deciding what to wear, it's better to be slightly overdressed than underdressed. When in doubt, choose an outfit that you can dress up or down with jewelry, a scarf, or a jacket. That said, the best thing is to determine in advance what clothing would be most appropriate for where you're going. Call your host or hostess, or, if it's a restaurant, poke your head in a few evenings before and check out what the patrons are wearing.

6. Make Sure Your Clothes Are Clean

This sounds so obvious, but it's important. Really check for subtle stains and spots. Sometimes you don't realize that you put your elbow in the chocolate mousse the last time you wore that sweater, or that a drip of coffee fell in the lap of those gray pants, or that your favorite white shirt has finally gotten too gray to wear. Check your shoes as well, making sure they're clean and polished.

7. Pay Attention to Your Grooming

Make sure your hair is well groomed (and not growing where it shouldn't) and your nails are clean and manicured. The last thing you need is a potential date staring at your fingernails while you talk. Pay attention to oral hygiene—there's no bigger turnoff than getting a waft of secondhand cabbage or cigarette breath. Be clean and sweet smelling, but don't overdo the perfume or after-shave. And remember, women generally have a better sense of smell than men.

Looking for Your Look

If you think your image or style (or lack of one) could do with a boost, then keep an active eye out for looks that might work for you. Begin by noticing what the people around you are wearing, paying particular attention to those whose style appeals to you. Take a look at catalogs and fashion magazines, do some window shopping, and browse clothing store racks. Start to notice which people on the street catch your eye—how are they dressed?

Choose clothes you feel comfortable in, but also that really flatter you and project the image of your best self. Some of us dress to blend in, and while that's okay, you can also add a little flair that expresses your personality and makes you feel adventurous. Sometimes an interesting accessory can add a little oomph and also be a conversation starter. For example, my wife wears hand-painted reading glasses and people are always asking her about them.

If you don't have a strong image of yourself and you feel you need help, hire a consultant or go to a good store (you

What Do Others See?

Think about your appearance and the clothes you wear;
then think about the image and attitude you'd like to project. Answer the following questions to help you determine
how your look can help you convey that image.

1. What aspect of my personality do I want to emphasize?
2. What do I want my appearance to communicate to others?
3. What changes must I make to achieve this?
4. What are the first steps I'll take toward accomplishing
my goal?

don't have to buy anything), try on stuff, and get opinions—
lots of them. Many high-end department stores provide in-house personal shoppers gratis. These people are there to
help you find the right look. Be sure to brief them well, giving them a sense of what type of person you are. The Wall
Street look may make you look dynamic in the mirror, but if
you're a sheep farmer it will eventually backfire because it's
not the real you.

The Total Package

In the world of advertising an "impression" is counted as
a single exposure to a product. Advertisers pay fortunes
to get their products out into the marketplace in the hope

that their low-fat waffles, turbocharged riding mowers, or irresistible lipstick flavors will garner lots of favorable impressions. They know that a good first impression means the difference between a consumer giving their product a try or giving it a pass.

Your irresistible first impression, your star power, is not going to be determined by TV commercials, glossy advertisements, or raving testimonials but by your attitude, your poise, and your wardrobe. Enhancing and focusing on these important aspects of your image will do more than boost your chances in the love market, it'll also boost the way you feel about yourself. When we feel good about ourselves it affects everything. We make better decisions, feel more adventurous, have more energy, and tap into our natural enthusiasm, all of which impacts the nonverbal signals we send out to others. Being on top of our game means others will want to join in and play.

hello,
how are you,
how do you do?

Studies by the Harvard School of Health Sciences and several other notable institutions show that we decide within *the first two seconds* of meeting people whether we like them or not. We make unconscious appraisals of their nonverbal signals based on our emotional and physical security: "I do/don't feel safe with you," "I do/don't trust you." Those assessments lead us to make snap judgments—right or wrong—about the people we encounter. If we like them, we tend to see the best in them; if we don't like them, we may well see the worst.

Since certain behaviors make people feel comfortable and others put them on guard, you actually have some measure of control over how people react to you in those first brief moments. Charming people look you in the eye when you first meet them; alarming people avoid eye contact or look at you so fleetingly that they seem shifty or nervous, and make you feel uncomfortable. Charming people smile when they meet you; alarming people have serious or worried mouths that set a disturbing tone. Charming people have open body language that says you're welcome to approach; alarming people have closed body language that says, "Scram, I've got better things to do."

Using Body Language to Build Trust

Let me describe a scene that took place last winter at my local ski hill. The players were Michelle, a friend of my youngest daughter, and Brad, a regular skier at the hill. Michelle worked at the ski shop, and Brad, a frequent customer, was attracted to her and was pretty sure she was eyeing him too. He wanted to approach her, and to do so came up with the ruse of signing up for an introductory snowboarding lesson. Let's look at both parties' body language, as the scene plays out.

Brad takes a seat across from Michelle at the sign-up desk, which is actually a small round table with a couple of chairs. While Michelle is arranging her papers, Brad hugs his shoulders, nibbles his lip a little, runs his tongue around his bottom lip, and looks down at the floor, occasionally sneaking glances at Michelle.

Michelle gets herself organized and faces Brad squarely and openly, her elbows on the arms of her chair, her forearms resting lightly and uncrossed on the table in front of her. She looks him in the eye and smiles as she explains the snow-boarding package, asking some questions and writing down the answers. Brad stops hugging himself and crosses his arms in front of his chest. His eyes dart around the room, rarely meeting Michelle's.

As she continues explaining the deal, Brad places his right elbow on the table and turns so his body is angled to the left, away from Michelle. He glances at her sideways and frequently looks away. She instinctively turns her body in the same direction as Brad's, and in a very natural move puts her left elbow on the table. They are almost mirror images of one another.

Brad seems to relax and appears to pay more attention to Michelle. After a few moments Michelle sits back in her chair and faces Brad directly. He does the same, but stuffs his right hand under his left armpit and covers his mouth with his left hand. Still, he's looking at her openly now and smiling a little. After a few moments Michelle mirrors Brad's arm and hand positions, then leans forward and says in a clear, calm, enthusiastic way, "The course starts next Saturday at nine." She uncrosses her arms and rests them once again on the table. Brad does the same, smiles, and asks, "So, after all these years of skiing, you think I'll be able to manage a board?"

They lock eyes and smile. "Sure," says Michelle, "and I think you'll have a really great time."

What Happened?

There was a lot going on in this little scene and we'll get to some of it in more detail in a later chapter, but basically Brad started out alarming, using closed body language. Michelle was charming and used open body language, and eventually her openness disarmed Brad and enabled him to relax. Michelle employed the three main behaviors that are essential when meeting a potential partner or, for that matter, anyone with whom you want to have a productive relationship.

1. Look the person in the eye.

2. Smile.

3. Open your body language
   (which I'll talk more about in a minute).

Let's look at these behaviors individually.

Windows on the Soul

How does it feel when you go into a store or a bank and the clerk never so much as looks at you? Or when you meet someone new and they look right past you, over your shoulder? The answer is simple: You feel slighted and probably form a negative impression of the person. That's because when there's no eye contact, trust and respect are absent.

We are born to make eye contact; it's the foundation for all social skills. According to new research by Dr. Teresa

Farroni of the Centre for Brain and Cognitive Development at England's Birkbeck College, babies as young as two days old can detect when somebody is looking directly at them. Not only that, but by the time they are four months old they show measurably more interest in faces that present a direct gaze than in those that are looking elsewhere. Being able to

> **Get in the habit of noticing the color of people's eyes when you meet them.**

make eye contact helps us establish human links and develop social skills, and is absolutely essential for forging relationships. Brad couldn't bring himself to look at Michelle until he was comfortable, and it limited his self-confidence and his ability to gain trust and respect. Michelle sought to make eye contact with Brad immediately, and it significantly enhanced her ability to make a connection.

Eye contact is intimate contact and, used properly, can create immense rapport and sexual intimacy. The easiest way to learn to consistently make eye contact is to get in the habit of noticing the color of people's eyes when you meet them. The color itself is unimportant, but it's a good device around which to build a new habit. Practice at the store, at work, and the next time you go to a restaurant. Practice with everyone you meet until it's second nature. Remember, you were born to make eye contact.

Smile and the World Smiles with You

Nothing says "I'm noticing you" the way eye contact does, and nothing says "I'm happy and confident" quite like a smile. A smile is good news all round, helping you present a better face (literally!) to the world and, in addition, acting as a pump for the neurotransmitter serotonin. When you smile, you tighten about 14 muscles at the corners of your mouth and ears, which causes an electrical message to be sent to your brain stimulating serotonin release, which gives you a sense of well-being. Go ahead, give it a try. You'll feel more attractive, capable, and satisfied.

As an added bonus, smiles, like attitudes, are contagious: If you smile at someone, in all likelihood she'll smile back, and get a nice little shot of serotonin perking up her system to boot. You've just made her feel good. Now wasn't that a cinch?

I know it sounds basic, but make a habit of looking people in the eye and smiling at them. It builds bridges. You'll get better service, make better friends, feel better about yourself, *and* be more attractive to potential partners.

Do you remember how you mentally yelled the word "Great!" three times in a row in the last chapter? Now say it out loud. When you do, you're obliged to tighten those same smile muscles around your jaw, making the serotonin flow. It's a trick I learned when I was a fashion photographer. Many models repeat the word over and over to themselves with conviction when they need to put on a genuine-looking smile. It works. So, next time you're going to meet someone, say "Great!" under your breath three times as you approach. By the time you get there you'll be smiling and feeling terrific.

The Broad Vocabulary of Body Language

Michelle and Brad from the ski shop are portraits of the two extremes of body language: open and closed. Michelle was open—her nonverbal gestures signaled cooperation, agreement, willingness, enthusiasm, and approval. Open body language says, "I'm comfortable with you." Brad's body language, on the other hand, was closed, and his nervousness showed in his unconscious defensive gestures. His body signaled resistance, frustration, anxiety, stubbornness, nervousness, and impatience, regardless of what he may actually have felt at the time. Closed body language says, "I'm uncomfortable with you."

Open Body Language

The simplest way to think about open and closed body language is that open body language exposes your heart (that is, your chest area and your face) and is welcoming. It shows trust and says, "Yes!" Closed body language defends your heart and, as you saw with Brad, it

No Gesture Is an Island

Individual gestures are the vocabulary of body language, just like the words on this page are the vocabulary of the book. By the same token, individual gestures convey no more meaning than would a single word on this page, in isolation; it's only when you combine them with other gestures and with a particular attitude that they start to tell a story. Also, a closed gesture, like Brad's hugging his own shoulders, could have been neutralized if he'd also been facing Michelle, looking her in the eye, and smiling. And sometimes body language tells a different story than what we imagine: Someone whose shoulders are tense may be in pain, and someone folding their arms over their chest may simply be feeling chilly!

can make you appear unfriendly, unhappy, angry, or aloof, no matter what your real feelings. It says, "No!"

Babies are great examples of open and closed body language. When they are comfortable, they lie on their backs with wide-open body language. When they're uncomfortable, they close up.

If you want to show someone that you're charming and not alarming, you have to open yourself up right off the bat, before you've even said a word. Presumably the attitude you've chosen will do this for you anyway. "Hi!" attitudes are open, just like Michelle's welcoming attitude. Open body language includes:

- Keeping your arms and legs uncrossed
- Facing the person with an easy physical attitude
- Maintaining good posture
- Leaning slightly forward, toward the person
- Keeping your hands open
- Keeping your shoulders relaxed
- Keeping your movements slow and relaxed
- Maintaining a generally comfortable aura

Open gestures are calm and deliberate. They are meant to be seen. When combined with open facial expressions (good eye contact and a smile), open body language signals trust, happiness, acceptance, and comfort, and sends the message that things are going well.

You can enhance your open signals with your clothing. Imagine spending half an hour at a café having coffee with someone who never unbuttons his or her coat. An open coat or jacket (or removing the garment entirely) exposes the heart literally as well as symbolically.

Positive, open body language and gestures reach out to others—they're the subconscious version of a good hug or a heart-to-heart talk.

Heart-to-Heart and Openhanded

The easiest and fastest way to demonstrate open body language and signal an open heart is to face the other person straight on—literally heart-to-heart. Think of it as having a spotlight in the middle of your chest, shining on the other person.

It's also a good idea to let the person see that you have nothing concealed in your hands—an instinctual worry that's been with us since caveman times. To put the person at ease, hold your hands in such a way that he or she can see them.

Closed Body Language

If open body language is like a warm hug, closed body language is like getting the cold shoulder. It's defensive and shuts people out. Closed gestures include:

- Avoiding eye contact
- Crossing your arms and/or legs
- Clenching your fists
- Turning your body at an angle to the other person
- Fidgeting
- Covering your mouth
- Moving stiffly or jerkily
- Maintaining a generally uncomfortable aura

Make a habit of opening your body language when you meet people. Stand and face them, notice the color of their eyes (to be sure you're making eye contact), smile, and shine your heart at them. You'll be amazed how these simple gestures build trust.

The Next Step: Talking!

Okay, all your nonverbal signals are in line: Your attitude is great, you're dressed so you feel and look good, and your body language is open. Now it's time to talk.

By far the easiest way to meet someone new is to be introduced formally. Then all that's required is for you to stick out your hand and say, "Janet, it's a pleasure to meet you." A good introducer will often say something that will help launch a conversation, such as, "Phyllis, meet Barry, my carpooling partner. Barry, meet Phyllis. Phyllis lives next door." This gives you a simple bit of information with which to start a conversation—it's a bit like kindling for a fire. Phyllis can now say to Barry something as simple as, "So you work downtown?" or as playful as, "You two drive together? Who gets to choose the radio station?" If Barry's the one to start the conversation, he can simply ask how long Phyllis has lived next door, or make a lighthearted jest about their host's skills as a neighbor. Let's take a closer look at another introduction to see how it works in more detail.

Making the Most of the First Few Moments

Tom, a mutual friend, introduces Karen and Patrick to each other when they both happen to be in his real estate office early one morning. Tom's a sociable guy and he knows how to make introductions, so the conversation starts flowing.

"I don't know if you two have ever met," he says. "Karen, this is my friend Patrick. We play tennis together, and I usually let him win! Patrick, this is my old friend Karen. We bumped into each other over the weekend. It must be five years at least since you left town for the high life, wouldn't you say?"

"About that," she replies. Then Karen turns to face Patrick, makes eye contact, smiles, and offers her hand. "Hello, Patrick, it's a pleasure to meet you."

Patrick looks Karen in the eye, smiles, shakes her hand (not too firm, not too limp), and says, "What a lovely way to start the day!"

Karen grins, "Thank you. Are you this charming on the tennis court?"

"Look," says Tom, "I just have to make a quick call. Why don't you two grab some coffee—it's freshly brewed—and I'll be right back."

"A lot can happen in five years," Patrick remarks as they move toward the coffeepot. "Where did you escape to?" His

tone is courteous, charming, and interested—he's been paying attention. "I hope you've been having fun."

"Most of the time. Being on call twelve hours a day and
dealing with really grumpy people may not be everybody's
idea of fun, but I love what I do."

"Coffee?" asks Patrick.

"Yes, please. Black."

"Let me guess. You're a doctor and you've been working
with the Peace Corps."

"You're a funny guy." Karen is laughing and relaxed.
"No, I'm not," she chuckles, "What about you? You're in
real estate, I guess."

Patrick shakes his head, "No. At least not in the way
you're probably thinking."

"You're a tennis pro?"

"Wouldn't that be nice!" Patrick laughs. "But now that
you mention it, what ball are we volleying here?"

"I don't know," Karen says coyly, looking at Patrick
over the rim of her coffee cup, "but it's fun."

You've heard the expression "Never look a gift horse in
the mouth"? In plain English, it means make the most of
your opportunities. Karen and Patrick were lucky that Tom
gave them something to work with when he introduced
them, and they were both paying enough attention to use the
information to banter back and forth and set a playful tone.
They also used body language, facial expressions, laughter,

feedback, and lightheartedness to fan the spark of an introduction into the flame of a conversation.

Both Patrick and Karen were ready, willing, and able to make the most of their first few moments. Karen exhibited a "you never know" attitude and chose an attractive, playful, and charming attitude, acknowledging the introduction, and making a great first impression. Patrick also did all the right things: He maintained Tom's upbeat and positive tone, then turned their first moments together into a game by riffing on the remark about Karen's five-year absence, introducing an air of mystery. He could have just laid all his cards on the table and said, "I have my own landscaping company and I'm here because Tom's introducing me to a new client. What do you do?" And then Karen could have told him she's a helicopter pilot who's been flying the frost patrol up north, and is here now to interview for City TV's traffic chopper job. Instead, they both chose play talk over small talk, and it made them appealing to each other.

Opening Lines

Suppose Tom hadn't paved the way for Patrick and Karen's conversation with his smooth social skills? Or suppose the phone had rung and he'd had to take the call, leaving them only knowing each other's names? In this kind of situation, there are three types of starters that either of them could have used to ease quickly and gently into rapport: a statement ("This is such a bright sunny office—I love the morning sun"); a question ("What brings you here so early in the morning?"); or a *sincere, pleasant* compliment. They could even try a mixture of all three.

Compliments are the riskiest because they're personal, and it's easy for them to seem opportunistic or smarmy. If Karen and Patrick had both had cameras hanging around their necks, it would be fine to say something like, "Wow, is that a 2.8 Tessar lens? That's gorgeous." But they are a man and a woman in a realtor's office, so unless Patrick could genuinely say something like, "That's a fresh cornflower in your lapel, isn't it? It's charming," he'd do better to choose another route to conversation.

> **Compliments only work when they are sincere and not fabricated for the moment.**

Compliments only work when they are sincere and not fabricated for the moment, and unless you're expert at delivering them, you run the risk of getting too personal too soon.

A statement followed by an open question is always a safe bet and a great way to start a conversation. You don't need to agonize over sparkling opening lines—they're just not worth it. The point of an opening line is to see if the person is interested in talking to you—it's an invitation to

Engineering Introductions

If a stranger across a crowded room catches your fancy, ask your host or a mutual friend or acquaintance to introduce you. But don't leave things to chance. Instead, prepare your own ten-second commercial ahead of time by telling your introducer what to say—your name, perhaps where you're from, and what you do for a living, or something else memorable about you, *all put in an interesting way.* It'll come off a lot better than "Heather, this is Jim. He got soaked coming here, didn't you, Jim?"

It's also important to follow that old rule: Two's company, three's a crowd. Politely ask your host to introduce

start up a conversation. Start with a statement (it could be about sports, the weather, the occasion, or the surroundings) and add a tag question (isn't it? don't they? doesn't she? etc.). "It's kind of cold tonight, isn't it?" The person will recognize this as a conversation starter and respond, especially if you look as if you expect a response. The way he or she responds will give you an idea of his or her willingness to continue the conversation. As a general rule, the longer and the more open the response, the better. Then, depending on the degree of the response, follow up with an open question: "How do you know Jack?"

you, say one or two interesting things about you, and then leave. "Heather, this is Jim. He lives in Seattle and he makes films." You want the third party out of the way so the conversation doesn't become two people talking and one listening—a bad dynamic for making a connection, no matter who ends up doing the talking.

If you really want to impress, ask your host to tell you two or three interesting things about the person you want to meet before he introduces you. Then, when you do connect, you can say, "Bob told me that you spent last month in a Buddhist retreat. What was it like? What inspired you to go?" This strategy puts you on a more personal footing faster.

Don't just take my word for it. Spend some time studying how the professionals do it on TV. Watch Oprah, Larry King, Barbara Walters, or Charlie Rose. They'll start with a quote, or a press clip, or a reference to a brewing scandal, then ask a question designed to elicit information (not just a yes or no answer).

A tip: Use the person's name within the first couple of minutes of meeting him or her. It has a magical effect. After all, a person's name is probably the most important word in the world to them. But do it subtly—you don't want to come off as the flashy salesperson type.

Free Information

Whether you're being introduced or are introducing yourself, the more information you have about the person you're meeting, the easier it is to get to know them.

In addition to paying attention and listening carefully, you can also encourage people to give you free information during an introduction. For example, if Clyde approaches a woman he doesn't know in a safe social situation and says, "Hi," there's a strong probability she'll say "Hi!" or something similar right back. But what if Clyde adds a tag of extra information to draw the woman into conversation? It could be something as easy as his name ("Hi, I'm Clyde.") or something more substantial. ("Hi, I'm Clyde Barrow from Teleco, Texas. This is my first time here.") Now the ball is in Bonnie's court and she'll either respond with her own information or Clyde can nudge her along with a few words ("And you are . . . ?") and/or an inquiring look or other body language.

Conversation is like a game of tennis. If you put the ball in the other person's court, that person usually knows to hit it back, and will do so naturally. If she doesn't, you can encourage her to. The point is that you've set the person up to reciprocate. Now you just have to wait for the ball to come back your way. What you end up with is information that can be used to escalate your conversation out of small talk into something more substantive.

approaching strangers

The setting in which you see someone can have a significant impact both on how you perceive each other and how you choose to approach him or her. In the best of all possible worlds there would always be someone available to make the introduction and a familiar, emotionally comfortable space within which to interact—a party, a dinner, a club meeting, or a class, for instance. Researchers call these settings *closed fields,* where everyone has the opportunity to meet and the expectation that they'll do so. Meeting people this way, with an introduction from a mutual acquaintance in a comfortable closed field, makes it more likely you'll share interests, values, and tastes, and also gives you an automatic conversational entrée, even if it's as simple as "How do you know Bob?" or "How did you get involved with this club?"

There are bound to be times, though, when you see someone you'd like to meet in a public *open field* like an airport, shopping mall, supermarket, or commuter train. For most of us, this can be a daunting situation. After all, from the earliest age our parents told us never to talk to strangers, and the mere thought of doing so immobilizes us. Let's make a new rule, though: While "don't talk to strangers" is a great watchword for kids, it's nonsensical for adults and is actually counterproductive. The ability to approach people in an easy, relaxed way is a valuable skill that can help in all areas of your life, whether you need a friend, a job, a shoulder to cry on, or someone to go on a cruise with you around the Cape.

No matter what the situation, there are two ways to approach strangers to whom you're attracted: the direct approach and the indirect approach.

The Direct Approach

Many of us go through life hoping that others will somehow intuit our desires and fulfill them without our having to articulate a thing. Sometimes we're even disappointed or feel rejected when people *don't* read our minds and provide what we want. The best way of getting what you want, though, is often just asking for it. Instead of simply noticing that cute guy or gal across the room and wishing he or she'd notice you back, now is the time to take action—to walk over and express your interest.

For most of us, this is scary. Unless you're a movie star, a model, or a notoriously wealthy bachelor or single woman, it takes a lot of guts to approach a stranger and start talking. But there are times when it's act now or never see the person again, or when the strength of your feelings overwhelms you and compels you to act—as was the case with a man I met, named Ryan.

A heavy equipment importer, Ryan was in Holland on business, riding a half-empty train from Amsterdam to The Hague. Sitting across the aisle from him were two attractively dressed women in their late thirties, roughly Ryan's age. They were speaking English, and Ryan couldn't help overhearing their conversation. One of them, an American, mentioned she was a journalist based in The Hague representing several overseas publications. The other, a young Indian woman dressed like a Wall Street executive, with a very correct English accent spiced with a hint of Indian pronunciation, worked for a British shipping line. Ryan told me the beauty of the Indian woman's voice mesmerized him. He sensed without any shadow of doubt that she was his type. "She talked slowly, choosing her words carefully and with precision. She was impeccably dressed—a little formal, totally classy."

> **Many of us go through life hoping that others will somehow intuit our desires and fulfill them without our having to articulate a thing.**

There were only two stops on the intercity express and from what he'd overheard, Ryan knew he'd be getting off before the two women. He felt so strongly attracted to this woman that he decided to do something about it. He told me he didn't feel inhibited; it was just something he had to do. Without giving himself time to talk himself out of it, he slid to the aisle end of his seat and, using open body language, a smile, eye contact, and a calm, confident voice, he addressed the journalist. "Hi. Excuse me." Then he turned to the other woman and, using a you-and-me gesture (*gently* pointing back and forth between her and himself), said, "Hello. Do you mind if I say something—something personal?"

"I don't know," the woman replied.

"It's just that as we've been moving along in the train for the last half hour and you were both lost in conversation, I couldn't help overhearing you." He paused to add tension. "I just want to say, you have the most beautiful voice."

She was gracious and relieved. "Thank you," she said.

"I find it *very* attractive." Ryan paused for a response, but as he expected, none was forthcoming. "I was wondering what you'd say if I invited you out for lunch?" he asked, nodding his head ever so slightly as if to say yes.

"I don't think so, but I'm very flattered," the woman replied. His opportunity was dissolving. The woman seemed genuinely amused at Ryan's advance, but shook her head as she said, "No."

"I'll tell you what," said Ryan. "Here's my business card. I'm going back to New York on Wednesday. Check out my Web site and you'll see I don't bite. Think about it—and when it's appropriate, give me a call. Or if you change your mind, or if you want to, you can e-mail me tonight. Maybe we can pencil in lunch tomorrow. Your choice." Still looking her in the eye, he smiled, then turned to the American journalist and said, "Thanks." He turned back to the woman with the enchanting voice and murmured, "Bye," then got up, scooted through the carriage doors, and got off the train at his stop.

Her name was Shantha. She called the next morning and they met for lunch around the corner from the Royal Palace in The Hague. "She made me feel like I could conquer the world," Ryan told his friends later. "He made me feel like the cleverest person he'd ever met," Shantha told her American journalist friend when she called for all the details.

Ryan and Shantha put an end to their long-distance relationship 18 months later when they got married and moved to the south of England.

The Direct Approach in Action

In 1989 the *Journal of Psychology and Human Sexuality* published the results of a study undertaken by Drs. Russell Clark and Elaine Hatfield called "Gender Differences in Receptivity to Sexual Offers." The researchers used average-looking male and female research assistants posing as regular students to approach attractive strangers of the opposite sex on a college campus and say, "I've been notic-ing you around campus. I find you very attractive." Then they'd randomly ask one of three questions to measure the gender differences in receptivity to sexual offers:

1. Would you like to go out with me tonight?

2. Would you like to come over to my apartment tonight?

3. Would you go to bed with me tonight?
   The results were predictable:

	Agreement by Respondents	
Question	Male	Female
1	50%	44%
2	69%	6%
3	75%	0%

Campus life is not exactly representational of society at large, but this does show that the direct approach to getting a date works about half the time with men and women alike—not a bad percentage, if you have the chutzpah to pull it off!

If you look at the wording the assistants used, you'll note that it begins with a location statement followed by a question that only requires a yes or no answer—not a very good idea. However, assuming you know how to be charming rather than alarming, "I've been noticing you around campus" (the office, the club, etc.) and "I find you very attractive" (or something about you—the way you dress, your voice, etc.) followed by, "How would you feel about meeting for a quick coffee at the end of the day?" stands a good chance of getting a positive response.

How Did He Do It?

Ryan travels on planes and trains often in the course of his business and doesn't make a habit of asking strange women out on dates. But this time it was different—his urge to talk to Shantha was so strong that he ignored the self-talk that would normally have told him not to be ridiculous. Something told him to go ahead and take action, and that allowed him to connect with his matched opposite.

Of course, it didn't hurt that three years earlier Ryan's boss had talked him into taking a course called Neuro-Linguistic Programming for Managers. Talking to Shantha, he used a few techniques he'd learned called "irresistible language patterns and gestures."

Pacing the Ongoing Reality

When Ryan introduced himself to Shantha, he used a technique that hypnotherapists call *pacing the ongoing reality*.

It's a great way to soften the impact of any approach, be it direct or indirect. In order to make you feel relaxed, a hypnotherapist will draw your attention to three *verifiables,* or things that are obviously true. Then, while you're in an agreeing frame of mind, they'll throw in a suggestion in the hope that you'll agree with that too. He or she might say, for example, "As you sit here (first verifiable), and listen to the sound of my voice (second verifiable), while you stare at the wall in front of you (third verifiable), you can begin to notice your shoulders are starting to relax and feel soft (suggestion)."

Go back and reread what Ryan said to Shantha. First he mentioned three things she had to agree with: yes, they were in a train; yes, it had been moving along for at least half an hour; and yes, she had been lost in conversation. All Ryan did was describe the situation and Shantha had to agree, albeit subconsciously, with what he was saying. He didn't say anything she could subconsciously refute. For example, he didn't say she was enjoying herself or that she found the seats comfortable—he'd have no idea whether either of those things was true.

Delivered with sincere body language and voice tone, this kind of language is irresistible, subtly putting people in a more open and relaxed frame of mind by giving them undeniable truths about their immediate environment.

Suppose, for example, you're waiting in line for a ride at Disneyland with your two young sons, and in front of you was an attractive guy with his two young daughters. You might casually say to him something like, "Just seeing all these people having fun, hearing them laugh, on such a beautiful day, it makes me feel good to be alive." The same approach would work on the patio of the Olive Garden or at the snack stand at the beach, assuming all your verifiables were verifiable and your children weren't driving everyone crazy! With or without a suggestion, this is a great way to get people to relax and set them up to agree with you.

Sleight of Head

You may have noticed that at one point Ryan also used something I call *sleight of head.* This involves using subtle body language to signal the answer you want to receive to a yes or no question. Flight attendants do this when they ask passengers, "Can I get you anything else?" If they want a yes answer, they nod ever so slightly "Yes" as they ask the question. If they prefer a no answer, they very subtly shake their head "No." As I mentioned earlier, consciously or not, we respond very profoundly to visual signals. When Ryan asked if he could ask Shantha out, he nodded "Yes" with the question, and although she initially turned him down, she may have been already having second thoughts.

Soft Questions

Soft questions, or *conversational postulates* to use their technical name, will typically get you a response without asking for it directly. If you ask someone a question like, "Do you know where the bus station is?" he or she won't normally reply "Yes" or "No," but will go ahead and tell you the location. If you read carefully, you'll see Ryan didn't actually come out and ask Shantha to have lunch with him; instead, he embedded his question in a statement about his own curiosity: "I was wondering what you'd say if I invited you out for lunch?" He asked a question without asking a question, which softened and distanced both it and the possible answer by making them hypothetical. "I'm curious to know what you would say if I asked you out." A slightly more direct version might be, "What would you say if I called you?" (or kissed you, etc.) This last is a real question, but it's still hypothetical and therefore somewhat removed and softened. Soft questions feel more natural than hard questions. They allow you to gently yet rapidly steer the conversation and appear more sensitive. In Shantha's case, she got the message and was flattered.

Influential Suggestions

Voice-over artists—the people who read advertising copy on TV and radio commercials—frequently use *influential suggestions* (also called *hidden directives* or *embedded commands*) to reinforce and direct the behavior of their audience. Persuasive communicators naturally do this all the time too. When Ryan said, "*Think about it—and when* it's appropriate, *give me a call.* Or if you *change your mind,* or if you want to, you can *e-mail me tonight,*" he was using influential suggestions to plant ideas. The secret is to mark the suggestions off from the rest of the sentence by changing your voice tone and body language slightly as you say them. Ryan paused ever so slightly before he said, "Give me a call" (and all the other imperatives in italics above) and shifted his voice tone down an increment, so as to be slightly more commanding. He also looked Shantha in the eye and was physically still, allowing her to focus entirely on his words.

> **Soft questions feel more natural than hard questions. They allow you to gently yet rapidly steer the conversation and appear more sensitive.**

Another form of suggestion comes from intentional ambiguity. Find something obvious you and someone you like have in common—let's say, tennis. You're going to say something like, "If you, like me, enjoy playing tennis, then you'll be interested in reading the new Monica Seles biography" (or whatever you want to add—"Check out the new clay courts on Route 16," or "You gotta try these new long-lasting balls"). This is a perfectly innocent comment, except as you say it you actually utter it like this: "If (very slight pause) you, like me (very slight pause), enjoy playing tennis, then you'll be interested. . . ." What happens is that the person you're saying it to takes in both messages (the instruction to like you and the actual conversational piece about tennis) without consciously realizing you slipped in a command. It's ten times easier than it sounds written down here. Give it a shot and practice marking off the command in a slightly more serious tone than the rest—and, of course, with eye contact. Once you get it, go back and reread Ryan's words to Shantha, marking the commands with the slightest pause and speaking them as instructions.

Whether or not you choose to use the direct approach, the above techniques are all useful, both in attracting and connecting with a person you're interested in and for communicating in general. In a matter of seconds Ryan made his move. Using verifiables, he paced the ongoing reality to gain acceptance and synchronize mentally with Shantha. He used soft questions and sleight of head to deliver his request, and employed influential suggestions to overcome her resistance.

Sure it's scary, and it's probably not the way to go for most of us, but if you can pull it off, the direct approach certainly cuts to the chase and saves time. Like most things, these skills get easier with practice. Practice them at work, at the hotel check-in, or when you're persuading the maitre d' to give you that table right in the middle of the action—

or, like Ryan and many of the thousands of people who have fallen in love at first sight, when you're spurred into action by being in the presence of your matched opposite.

The Indirect Approach: Assuming Rapport

Have you ever been at a gathering and had someone come up to you and say something relatively innocuous, and the next thing you know you're chatting like old friends? If so, you've just had someone assume rapport with you. It's a nice easy feeling and it's how the socially gifted make the most of their initial connections. They simply walk up to the person with whom they wish to connect and, usually without so much as a hello, carry on as if they'd known them all their life. Sure, it requires a certain amount of bravado, but with practice you can get quite comfortable with it.

Assuming rapport is a subtle, less intrusive way to connect with a person you're interested in. It's less emotionally risky than the direct approach because it doesn't require any kind of introduction and outright request. You simply turn up, note something interesting that's going on at that moment, and begin your conversation in the middle: "Chocolate-covered orange peel is just decadence itself. How do you think they ever came up with an idea like

Asking for a Date

If you have assumed rapport and it's going well *and there is chemistry on both sides,* there's nothing to stop you asking for a date right there and then. Whether you're a man or a woman, all you need to say is, "I really enjoyed talking [chatting, comparing notes, running around in the rain, etc.] with you, and it would be great if we could get together again sometime," then wait for an answer. Say nothing. Let the soft question/conversational postulate work it's magic for you. The options are that he or she will either accept or decline. If the answer is yes, then make a date immediately or exchange phone numbers and say when you'll call. If the answer is no, it will either be flat out or come with an excuse. Excuses usually revolve around availability or time: "I'm happily married," "I'm in a relationship," or

that?" Or, "Turner's paintings have this amazing mystery to them. What do you think he was trying to say?" Or, "There must be more ice cream trucks in this part of town than in the rest of the state combined. Why do you think that is?"

One of the main advantages of assuming rapport is that you get to check someone out before deciding to make a move. You can chat with them a little in a normal, innocent, upbeat way and see if you hit it off. First impressions can be

"I'm tied up for a while." Assume that when an invitation is declined, the interaction is over. In other words, assume that no really does mean no.

The business of a woman asking a guy out is to some degree a generational thing: The younger you are, the more acceptable it is; the older you are, the more it might make either or both of you uncomfortable. But, gals, whatever your age, I think you'll be amazed how many guys will be flattered, relieved, and impressed that you made the effort. And honestly, what have you got to lose? If you're really nervous, turn it around and be playful: "I had a great time talking with you," you can say, "and I think it'd be great if you asked me out." If your rapport has been really good and he looks to be getting the hint, you could even reinforce it with some fun body language, like smiling, widening your eyes expectantly, and nodding your head "yes."

deceiving. That attractive guy nursing his double espresso and staring out of the window at Starbucks may not turn out to be the Parisian poet you imagined but a charter member of gamblers anonymous who hasn't bathed in a month. That goofy-looking girl in the granny glasses at Grand Central may turn out to be a sexy Broadway dancer rather than a hippie wallflower. You never know! Assuming rapport gives you room to explore.

An example: Henry sees an appealing woman having lunch up at the counter in a busy restaurant and sits down next to her. He picks up the menu, studies it for a moment, then, with all innocence and openness, as if he were an old friend or a cousin, he leans over and asks, "What do you recommend? I've never eaten here before." If her reply is a recommendation, it's terrific and he takes it from there. If it's "Neither have I," that's wonderful too. Either way, they have something in common.

> The idea behind assuming rapport is that you don't use any particular opening line—you just start talking.

Francine is at her cousin's wedding. After the ceremony, as the bride and groom are getting into their limo to head for the reception, the skies open and it starts to pour. Francine turns to the attractive guy next to her, looks him in the eye, shrugs, and lets out a laugh. "What are we going to do now?" she asks him.

"I don't know," he says.

"Let's run for it," she says. "Where are you parked?" They're both soaked, they must have mutual friends since they're attending the same function, and they're both running to the parking lot. They have plenty in common.

Ashley has come to check out the natural gas fireplaces at the Fireside store. She's deep in thought, imagining how the latest Vermont Majestic will look in the farmhouse she's renovating. Marty turns up next to her, brochure in hand, and studies the freestanding stove two models away from Ashley's Majestic.

"Do you think these stoves look more authentic in black, or do you think the colored ones still give that country look?"

Ashley looks up. "Excuse me?" Marty repeats the question.

Ashley laughs. "You must be a mind reader," she says. "I was just wondering the same thing."

They spend the next five minutes exchanging opinions, giving each other free information. They have lots in common.

How to Assume Rapport

The idea behind assuming rapport is that you don't use any particular opening line—you just start talking. The more you learn to include details about whatever's going on around you at the time, the more relaxed and natural you'll appear. Be relaxed and natural. This is supposed to feel like the opposite of a come-on or pickup. *Casual* is the keyword. It's perfectly natural and friendly to exchange a few words with people in your daily comings and goings. This kind of friendly chitchat can happen in line at the supermarket, at a cocktail party, at a ballgame, at an airport waiting lounge, an art gallery—you name it.

So, how do you go about feeling casual, relaxed, and natural as you assume rapport? Simple: The key is to practice. Any of the following types of statements, questions, or compliments will do to get you started:

- An open question (i.e., one that can't be answered by a simple yes or no), such as, "So, what have you heard about this movie?"

- An occasion/location statement, which refers to what's going on around you as well as to where you happen to be (e.g., the market). For example, "At last, fresh pineapple."

- An occasion/location statement, followed by an open question: "At last, fresh pineapple. How can you tell if it's ready to eat?"

- A remark: "Oh, wow, I've got my watch set to the wrong date!"

- An observation: "Woo hoo! Looks like our team's going to win tonight!"

- A sincere compliment: "I have to tell you, I just love your hat!"

- A request for an opinion: "I've never eaten here before. Is there anything you recommend?"

Assuming Rapport

Read the following scenarios and, using the details of the situation, just assume you have rapport and decide what you would say. Come up with a conversational statement for each, and follow it with an open question.

1. It's raining as you leave the store. Several people are waiting for the rain to let up a bit because they, like you, have no umbrella. You are standing near someone you find attractive, and you say . . .

2. You're at work, and walk outside for your break because it's a beautiful afternoon. You notice someone you don't know, who works in another department. You approach and say . . .

3. On your way to work you stop at a convenience store for a cup of coffee and notice an attractive person getting ready to pour a cup too. You say . . .

4. You're trying on shoes and someone you find attractive is standing near you, holding a pair of sneakers and waiting patiently for the salesperson to reappear . . .

Assume the Best

When you spot someone you fancy, don't start making assumptions about how he or she will feel if you approach. You have no idea whether they'll be embarrassed, offended, or thrilled to bits, so just approach and see what reaction you get. You have nothing to lose. The worst you can expect is a little dent in your ego.

If you have to make an assumption, *assume it will work.* Assume that others will give you the benefit of the doubt and do the same with them. Assume they will be influenced by your positive outlook and attractive attitude. Most people are eager to connect and to be friends with us, so assume the best.

That said, it's also wise to remember that we're all more open and receptive to talking to strangers at some times than at others. Sometimes we just feel like keeping to ourselves— maybe we've had a hard day, or have something important on our minds, or any of a million other reasons we may just want to be left alone. When we're in this state of mind, often we emit signals—a preoccupied or troubled expression, for example, or other closed body language. It's smart to be on the lookout for such signals (and for their opposite, for receptivity) before you approach. If you approach and sense any stiffening or annoyance, or the person simply ignores you, that's okay. Just smile, excuse yourself, and go about your business. You've been friendly. Leave it at that.

The Three-Second Rule

The longer you put something off, the harder it is to do it. Did you ever miss out on an opportunity because you were too slow off the mark? Or talk yourself out of doing something and then regret it later? Have you ever sat in a bar nursing a glass of wine or beer all night, watching other people enjoy themselves while you never budge or make a move? "I'll just order one more drink, then I'll go for it." "Next time she looks this way, I'll smile at her." "Maybe that new guy that just walked in is more my type." Then you end up disappointed with yourself at the end of the night because you talked yourself out of something or just plain chickened out.

> When you spot an opportunity that's too good to pass up, don't: Just count to three, adjust your attitude, and make your approach.

Were you hoping, consciously or unconsciously, that if you hung around long enough something might just happen on its own? This is the social equivalent of putting your dirty dishes in the sink and hoping they'll wash themselves. Opportunities multiply as they are seized. What if you had approached all those people? By now, you might have a whole new social network. One of those folks at the bar might have taken you to a barbecue, and there you might have met a gal who invited you to go to a play, and her brother might have come along, and he might have brought a buddy who in turn might have invited you to go sailing with him and his friends. And the next thing you know, you could've been hosting a potluck for 16 great new people, one of whom could easily be your matched opposite.

But if you just hang around wishing, waiting, and hoping for something to happen, nothing ever will. The more you wait, the greater the chance that the guy you have your eye on will leave, or someone else will join that cute blonde woman for a conversation. Then you'll have even more reason to beat yourself up for procrastinating.

Remember the advice Christina, the horsewoman, gave Laura when she was new in town in chapter 3: three seconds. Make your move within three seconds. Seize the moment and take action.

Most people are eager to connect, and nothing's sadder than two lonely people coming within greeting distance of one another without either of them taking the opportunity to offer a word, build a bridge, or signal his or her interest. They pass each other on the street, sit next to each other in cafés, and see each other every day as they go about their lives. They may be longing to connect, but nothing is going to happen until somebody makes an effort. So, when you spot an opportunity that's too good to pass up, don't: Just count to three, adjust your attitude, and make your approach.

You can use a direct approach, like Ryan on the train. If you have the confidence, this is a great way to get things going. Or you can use the indirect approach and assume rap-

The Three-Second Rule

EXERCISE

Today, go out and assume rapport with three strangers. We're going to start small, so choose three people who aren't intimidating in any way. The goal is simply to say something to a stranger, not to start a conversation. You can say whatever you'd like, but statements are the easiest—just some remark about the location or occasion. Of course, you should adjust your attitude, open your body language, and be charming. This is a given for any encounter. But here's the important part of this exercise: You are going to make your way over to the person the moment you spot them. In your head you will count to three, then go over without hesitation.

You are creating a new habit, with "one, two, three" as your trigger. Practice, practice, practice—just do it. The key point is that you'll get comfortable breaking the ice and taking action. The more you practice chatting with strangers, the easier it will become.

port. Assuming rapport has three advantages: It is noncommittal, it allows you to learn a little about the person, and it enables you to make a face-saving exit should the encounter not bear fruit. After all, assuming rapport is first and foremost a casual approach, so a casual exit is perfectly okay.

Casually turn up next to someone you're interested in, wait a respectful half minute or so (in this case the three-second rule applies to moving in, not to choosing the moment to engage), then just start talking as if you're talking to your cousin or an old friend. Be sure to avoid giving the impression you're hitting on the person. Just be confident, interesting, and, if possible, amusing. The key is to be as casual, relaxed, and confident as you can.

If there's chemistry and you have a comfortable opportunity to ask for a date, that's fabulous. If there's no chemistry, just move on. But, if there does seem to be chemistry but you're stymied after the initial approach, you may need to tune up your conversational skills. In the next chapter, we'll take a look at how to fan the sparks you've already kindled into a flame.

PART 3

go!

Put it all together—move from

connection to intimacy to love in

90 minutes or less.

conversation and chemistry

Okay, you've made the initial contact. You've approached or been introduced or flirted and said "Hi," and you've felt a little chemistry, or perhaps a lot—enough to suggest that this could just be a matched opposite for you. Now, how are you going to keep it going? How are you going to move from introductory remarks to an engaging conversation? Too often a promising introduction, a good first impression, or a smooth approach fizzles because neither person knows quite what to say next. They can't get past small talk to more interesting, substantive conversation, where real connections are made.

As you already know, questions are the spark plugs of conversation. Almost everybody likes to talk about themselves (and those who don't, usually like to talk about what they know), so if you ask good questions, you're halfway there. I say halfway, because the other important component to good conversation is careful listening. Sometimes we're so involved in making sure that we hold up our end of the talk that we only

Online vs. In Person

Part of the reason Internet dating is so popular is that it doesn't happen in real time—you don't get flustered by someone looking at you, and you can rewrite your answers until they sound witty and interesting. Not so in real life. With someone watching, you can't close your eyes to think, screw up your face in search of a brilliant thought, or chew on the back of your knuckles looking for that perfect nugget of wisdom. For many people, conversations on the phone are easier than talking in person, too. However, as many of the people who initiate their relationships online will tell you, "It was all pretty wonderful until we

half pay attention to what the other person is saying. But active listening—when you pay attention and really respond to the person with whom you're talking—is critical to a meaningful connection. Good questions paired with active listening is an almost foolproof recipe for a lively, engaging conversation.

It's All in the Asking

It's amazing how people will blossom when you ask them a question about something for which they care deeply. But questions can also be seen as intrusive or nosy, so it's a actually met face-to-face; then I knew immediately there was no chemistry."

When you come face-to-face, you're bombarded by sensory input: You can see, hear, feel, and smell the person. These are the elements for real chemistry, and when it's there, you just know it. Close your eyes and think of three people, of either sex, with whom you have chemistry. I'll bet conversation with these people is fairly effortless, right? Ditto when it comes to making someone fall in love with you. Conversation without chemistry won't lead you to long-term romance; conversation with chemistry will. The greater the chemistry, the more effortlessly the conversation flows.

good idea to start off gently, with neutral questions, such as: "How do you know our host?" "Is this your first time here? How do you like it?" "What do you think about Jack's paintings?" You don't want to start off by grilling people or digging into their personal lives; all you want to do is get the ball rolling. When they respond, pay attention to both their answers and their body language, which will give you clues as to their comfort level. If they make eye contact, appear relaxed, sit facing you, and smile, it's likely they're comfortable with you.

The Building Blocks of Active Listening

In the *Journal of Research of the University of Maine,* Dr. Marisue Pickering identified ten discreet skills for active or empathetic listening.

1. *Attending and acknowledging:* Providing non-verbal awareness of the other person through eye contact and physical feedback.

2. *Restating and paraphrasing:* Responding to the person's basic verbal message.

3. *Reflecting:* Revealing feelings, experiences, ideas, or thoughts of your own that parallel what the other person has said or hinted at through non-verbal cues.

Quality Questions

There are two kinds of questions: open and closed. Closed questions generally begin with "Are you," "Have you," or "Did you," and they enable you to respond with a one-word answer. Think about it. If I say to you, "Are you a fan of Julia Roberts?" all you really have to say is yes or no.

Open questions usually begin with who, what, why, where, when, or how, and require more than a monosyllabic

4. *Interpreting:* Offering a tentative interpretation about the other's feelings, desires, or meaning.

5. *Summarizing and synthesizing:* Bringing feelings and experiences together; providing a focus.

6. *Probing:* Supportive questioning that requests more information or attempts to clear up confusion.

7. *Giving spoken feedback:* Sharing perceptions of the other's ideas or feelings; disclosing relevant personal information.

8. *Supporting:* Showing warmth and caring in one's own individual way.

9. *Checking perceptions:* Finding out if interpretations and perceptions are valid and accurate.

10. *Being quiet:* Giving the other person time to think as well as to speak.

answer. They tend to get people to open up. For example, "What do you think of Julia Roberts?" or "What do you do for fun?" However, the key is to pick up on something they say or something that's going on around you, rather than ask a question out of left field. "Oh, look at that enormous dog! And that woman walking him couldn't weigh more than a hundred pounds. How do you think she controls him?"— that kind of thing.

But your questions don't even have to be very clever or well thought out. My personal favorites are, "Tell me about _____" and "What do you think about _____?" These two phrases are really instructions for the other person to start talking, and they're almost fool-proof. Try it the next time you talk to someone: Ask him or her to tell you about something, then respond by looking and sounding interested and paying attention to all the conversational pointers that flow out of them (see below). It's that simple. Add some feedback and some questions based on things they've said, and if there's chemistry, who knows where it might lead. As I mentioned in the previous chapter, it's gentler to preface your question with a statement that reflects a common interest, something about the meeting or party you're attending, some fascinating current event—even the weather will do in a pinch. Follow this remark with an open-ended question: "This place gets the greatest bands. What's your favorite kind of music?" Then pay attention to the answer you get.

Pointing the Way

An important part of paying attention is listening for *pointers*. Pointers are little tidbits of information that lead you to possible avenues of conversation and also enable you to learn more about the person with whom you're speaking.

Jack literally bumps into Jill at a country fair and says, "So sorry! Are you okay? I'm looking for someone so I wasn't watching where I was going. I'm really sorry."

Jill, noticing that Jack is attractive, replies, "I'm fine. Do you need help finding anything?"

"I have a friend who lives in town. I promised to pick up some odds and ends and drop them off for auction. He left a note saying he was here, so here I am. But I can't find him."

"There are food tents over there," she says pointing behind Jack, "and the tractor pull is over there."

Whoa! Jill literally missed the point(ers)! Jack offered her two tidbits of free information as he lobbed the conversational ball over the net, but instead of returning his serve, Jill did the conversational equivalent of putting her racket down and biting her fingernails. She should have said something like, "So there's an auction coming up? Do you know when?" and/or "Sounds like you're from out of town. How well do you know our little village?"

> **It's important to not only ask questions but also to volunteer free information.**

Pointers are usually words you can pick up and repeat back to your conversational partner to steer and focus the conversation. Just choose the pointer that seems the most obvious, or the one that interests you the most, and let it take the conversation in that direction. Also, take a leaf out of Jack's book and drop a few nuggets of free information. It's important to not only ask questions but also to volunteer free information. That way people will get to know you and you can learn a little about them, too, without making them feel like they're being grilled.

Paying Attention

There are great TV interviewers and lousy ones. The lousy ones either ask bland, formulaic questions or they talk more than the guest does. The great ones are skilled, active listeners.

The ground rules for active listening and connecting successfully in conversation are pretty much the same as for interviewing: Establish rapport, ask questions to get the person talking, pay attention to their answers, follow their pointers, and give feedback. Active listening is a terrific way to open people up and get them to reveal more about themselves than they might normally.

In conversation (even with friends and family), most people consciously or unconsciously want to come off as intelligent, powerful, important, or valued, so we feel we have to defend and justify our ideas and beliefs. Because of this, we spend more time thinking about what we're going to say next than we do listening to what the other person is saying, and conversations can devolve into two defensive people sparring awkwardly with each other. This can be avoided by demonstrating to the other person, by careful listening, that you really care about what they are saying. You're putting them at ease and giving them validation, so they're more likely to explain in detail how they feel and why. Active listening thus becomes a prerequisite for emotional intimacy.

Conscious Feedback: Give It, Get It

Connecting is a two-way arrangement in which the participants cooperate and encourage each other along. If you look and act interested, I assume you are interested. If you don't react or respond, I assume you're not interested in talking to me at all. Your behavior will then become a self-fulfilling prophecy: People won't want to spend time with you and you will, in fact, end up being alone.

People who don't give feedback appear bored, boring, or baffling, so maximize how you listen and respond to others, using your whole face and body to show your interest. Start with your eyes and mouth, using them to register your feelings—surprise, delight, disgust, whatever. But don't stop there. Shrug your shoulders, throw your hands in the air, laugh, cry—respond! Lean forward in your seat, using your posture to show you're paying attention. Nod your head and encourage the other person verbally as well with interjections like "You're kidding!" "He said *what?*" or "That's amazing." And don't forget to use the power of silence.

175

Give the other person time to think as well as to talk. As I mentioned earlier, it's instructive in this regard to watch how talk show hosts (and, for that matter, any people you admire for their social skills) create chemistry with their questions and their active listening.

Also work on your ability to read others' feelings through their body language and facial expressions. Some of us are instinctually better at this than others, but the more you hone your sensory acuity, the more you'll be able to steer conversations and situations into areas of comfort and relaxation. If you're rambling on about your yachting adventures and don't notice that the very thought is making your listener seasick, your feedback skills need work. Ditto if you've cornered someone you're attracted to and can't sense that he or she is uncomfortable because you're standing too close. (For more on this, see the exercise on personal space in chapter 8.)

> **People who don't give feedback appear bored, boring, or baffling.**

The "Me Too" Trigger

Do you know the feeling of satisfaction you get when someone really understands you, when you spill your guts about something that's dear to your heart and your listener says empathetically, "I feel that way, too" or just

"Me too"? That kind of "Me too" empathy is one of the most powerful triggers you have to connect with others and cement the sense that you're sharing common ground. So, in every one of your interactions—be it flirting at a bar or a conference, assuming rapport at a party or the laundry, or out on a date—always be on the lookout for opportunities to honestly say, "Me too." You're saying, "See, we're alike," and reinforcing the matched part of the matched opposites concept. It also means you've found a good pointer to follow toward deeper conversation and connection.

Practice finding opportunities to say "Me too." Simply pay attention to what's being said and when the opportunity arises, jump in and say it—as long as it's true. "I love hot dogs." Me too. "I had to park miles away." Me too. "I can dance the polka after a couple of beers." Me too.

Let's look at another, more everyday conversational scenario.

Ian arrives at the bank to make a deposit ten minutes before it's due to open. It's a beautiful crisp spring morning and the downtown traffic is in full rush hour mode. He picks up a coffee from the shop directly across from the bank and wanders into the small park next door to wait for the bank to open. There are two benches, one free, the other taken by a pretty young woman in a green jacket and a dark skirt. Ian puts his backpack on the empty bench, flips his stirring stick into a garbage can, and casts a sidelong glance at the woman.

He's found himself in this type of situation more often than he cares to remember, seeing someone attractive and wanting to approach, yet scared stiff at the prospect. This time, he reminds himself that all he wants to do is start a conversation, get the young woman talking, and see if she wants to be friendly. With his heart pounding he walks up to the bench and says the most obvious thing he can think of.

"Hi. Do you mind if I sit here?"

The woman moves slightly to her left. "No, I don't mind," she murmurs, and Ian sits down.

Always be on the lookout for opportunities to honestly say, "Me too."

"What a beautiful morning. I'm waiting for the bank to open. Are you in line before me, for the bank?" he asks jokingly.

"Not really. I'm just starting work with a travel agency up there on one of the floors, so I got here early."

"This isn't a bad area to work in. There are quite a few good restaurants around the block. I work in that building over there."

Ian missed out on the pointers—first day, working for a travel agent. He should have picked up on these nuggets and used the who, what, where, why, when, and how conversation starters: "How long have you been in the travel business?" "What will you do there?" Or he could have just said, "First day—are you nervous?" He ignored one of the golden rules of connecting: Pay attention. Did you spot the near perfect opportunity for a "Me too" moment that he missed when she said she got there early? He should have said, with humor and enthusiasm, "Oh yes, me too."

All right, let's try it from a woman's point of view.

Tina, a pharmacist, is on an Alaskan cruise with her friend Jasmine. One morning, out for a stroll around the deck on her own, Tina sees an attractive man seated on a bench. She sits down beside him and notices he's reading the latest John Grisham novel. Grisham is her favorite author! He smiles at her as she sits, and knowing that they have the book in common, she smiles back.

But the man has gone back to reading. Tina decides to plunge ahead.

"So, are you a Grisham fan?"

"Not really," says the man. "This is the first book of his I've ever read."

"Oh really, why's that?"

"I don't get much time for reading. In my line of work the hours can get pretty unpredictable."

"Well, I've read all his books. He's one of my favorite authors, although I also like Nora Roberts a lot, too. She goes backwards and forwards between mystery and romance."

What response can Tina expect? First she makes a mistake by asking a closed introductory question (she was just lucky that he volunteered more); then the last thing out of her mouth is a series of statements, not questions. Tina was on track with her second query, a why question, but then she ignored the free information that he gave her in reply, and went on to talk about herself. If she'd been paying attention, she would have followed up with, "What is it that keeps you so busy?" then looked for pointers in his answer that would have led to further conversation. Or she could have said, "Tell me about your hectic life," or "Well, what do you think of Grisham so far?"

By now I've drummed into your head that occasion/location statements, open questions, pointers, feedback, paying attention, and "Me too" triggers are the staples of conversation. But it's going to take something more to sail you smoothly into conversation *and* chemistry. There's one really powerful tool that we haven't yet mentioned that you can use to make someone feel comfortable, help the conversation flow, and create chemistry. It's called synchronizing, and it's arguably the most powerful of all the rapport skills.

Getting in Synch

Have you ever noticed that couples who feel comfortable in each other's company tend to speak and sit the same way? They lean, nod, and readjust their position the same way; talk at the same speed, volume, and pitch; and use a lot of the same words and phrases. What they're doing is synchronizing with each other, a process that produces and reinforces the kind of natural harmony and trust that's a prerequisite for emotional intimacy. Perhaps they both speak in quiet tones, leaning toward each other with their arms resting on the dining table, picking up each other's rhythms and nods and smiles—basically reflecting one another.

Let's look at an example. I was thrilled to receive this note from a professional woman who had purchased my first book, though it wasn't the kind of book she normally went for. ("Somehow it just leaped out at me and I bought it.") In the moments before she left for a first date, she'd read through the section on synchronizing. Here are her words: "After dinner we went to a concert, and I focused on synchronizing his body language during the second half of the concert. Much to my surprise, sexual sparks started flying toward me . . . and I later found out that the sparks were mutual. He told me that he found me seductive. The truth is, what he found seductive was the synchronization!" Sexual sparks—sounds like chemistry to me.

If you look back at Michelle's interaction with Brad at the ski shop in chapter 5, what she was doing was synchronizing his body language: When he moved into a certain position, she easily and naturally did the same. When we're feeling comfortable, most of us do this naturally. But Michelle wasn't only synchronizing with Brad; she was taking it a stage further and using her own body language to lead Brad into a more comfortable state. Go back to page 124 and read the anecdote again to see how smoothly she did it.

Matching and Mirroring

Synchronizing includes *matching,* which means doing the same thing as the other person (she moves her left hand, you move your left hand) and *mirroring,* which means, as it implies, you move as though you were watching the other person in a mirror (he moves his left hand, you move your right). You'll tend to use matching when you're sitting or walking *next to* someone, and mirroring when you're *facing* him or her. Synchronizing doesn't mean mimicking, however. This isn't a game of Monkey See, Monkey Do. Your movements must be subtle and respectful. If your conversational partner is facing you across a table at the little French bistro and leans onto her right elbow, you lean on your left elbow—mirror image. If you're both leaning against the rail on the ferryboat admiring the sunset and she rests on her elbows and crosses her legs, you do the same—matching. If you're sitting side by side at a concert or a movie and she leans in toward you, you lean in toward her. These are the kinds of nonverbal signals you'll be relying on a great deal to accelerate feelings of comfort and closeness as you get emotionally intimate with your matched opposite.

Maybe you're thinking, "But won't other people notice that I'm copying their behavior?" Actually, they won't, unless the copying is blatant. If someone sticks a finger in his ear and you do the same, then yes, he'll probably notice that. But when a person is focused on a conversation, he or she will not pick up on sensitive synchronizing. So-called socially gifted people synchronize with others naturally all the time without thinking. Just do the minimum necessary to feel it working—and you certainly will.

Think of synchronizing as you and the other person each rowing your own boat, but doing so in tandem, side by side. You point your boats in the same direction, and pick up on each other's pace, stroke, breathing pattern, point of view, and body movements in order to maintain the same speed and course. Eventually, as Michelle did, you'll be able to use these to lead the other person where you want him or her to go.

You can synchronize any or all of the following—and the more the better:

• Body position and movements

• Head tilts

• Facial expressions

• Mental attitude

• Tone and volume of voice

• Rate of speech (speaking faster/slower)

• Breathing

The Hunt for Common Ground

While "Me too" moments enhance closeness, and synchronizing body language enhances trust and chemistry, the realization that two people share things in common (favorite movies, vacation places, restaurants, TV shows, sports, hobbies) makes them feel that they already know and understand quite a lot about each other and can find plenty to talk about in a more relaxed and natural way. If they decide to date, it also helps them choose events and activities that will be enjoyable and memorable for both of them.

Relieving the Pressure

I was able to demonstrate the incredible usefulness of discovering common ground to several hundred thousand people when I appeared on a CBS television special about speed dating. In case you aren't familiar with it, speed dating began as a way for Jewish singles to meet each other. In one evening, participants meet seven people of the opposite sex in individual one-on-one conversations for seven minutes each. If a person feels that he would like to see one of his dates again, he simply writes yes on a secret ballot; if both people feel this way, the organization puts them in touch. There are now countless variations on this idea.

On this particular show, a young woman had three "speed dates" with three different bachelors. To make it more exciting, the participants were only given 60 seconds to strut their stuff. My job was to advise and guide them as the show progressed. The first bachelor, a well-dressed and well-meaning fellow, spent his 60 seconds nervously avoiding eye contact, hardly ever managed a smile, and kept his heart pointed away from the woman—and he did all the talking to boot. The second willing lothario implemented the suggestions I gave him about eye contact, smiling, and body language, and asked his partner questions to get her talking. This was clearly progress, and the studio audience could definitely sense the improvement.

My main suggestion to the third bachelor was to follow the previous guy's lead, but also find some interest he and the woman shared in common. He succeeded big time. Within 15 seconds they discovered they both enjoyed skydiving. The sense of relief was enormous. Their body language relaxed, they smiled a lot and had tons to talk about. What was probably most palpable was the reaction from the studio audience. They collectively synchronized with the connected couple, leaning forward, looking enthusiastic, and smiling among themselves.

Conversation: The Original Information Society

It is through conversation that relationships take root and blossom. It is through conversation and chemistry that enduring romantic relationships take root, blossom, and

(continued on page 188)

Synchronizing Your Way to Great Rapport

Of all the exercises in this book, the next one is the easiest to learn, and without a doubt, the most powerful when it comes to helping you put another person at ease. It's also one of the best ways to recover from a less than perfect first impression and restore comfort and trust.

A word of warning here: Time and again people come up to me when I give speeches and say they'd tried out this exercise after hearing me describe it in a previous talk, and had started to crack up laughing when they realized how easy it was to make it work. Put on your poker face!

Here's the story: In my workshops I invite a volunteer onto the stage and ask him or her to sit in one of two chairs that are facing each other about seven feet apart. Once the person has taken his seat, I sit down in the other seat and mirror his position. If his legs are crossed, I cross mine; if he's leaning slightly sideways, I do the same thing—mirror style. If he nods slightly and smiles, I do the same. We're in synch, and it's natural. Then I ask him to stand and lean on the chair in any way that's comfortable. He does so and I do the same—and that's natural too. From there we chat for five or ten seconds, then I'll fold my arms and guess what? He folds his, too.

I'll cross my legs and guess what? He crosses his, too—and the audience laughs because they notice it, even though he doesn't. We are in the zone—synchronized, relaxed, and trusting.

Part 1: Synchronize Body Language
For one day, make it a point to synchronize the overall body language of the people you meet. You don't have to let on what you're up to, just enjoy the experience. With each person, be aware of their shoulders, arms, legs, and torso and begin with the bigger movements—crossing arms or legs, leaning forward or back, etc. This is the fastest way to build trust and communication. Just remember not to overdo it. *Do as little as you need to adjust to the other person.*

Part 2: Make and Break Synchronizing
Once you become good at synchronizing overall body language—and one day should make you an expert—practice synchronizing with someone for about 30 seconds, and then breaking synchronization for 30 seconds (stop matching and mirroring the person, and use your body and voice differently from the way they're using theirs), then resynchronizing. Go through the cycle a few times. You'll be able to feel the trust, concentration, and intimacy level drop significantly as you break synchronization, and return in a big way when you resynchronize.

(continued from page 185)

bear fruit. When chemistry is absent, no matter how valiant the effort, it's still an uphill and often useless battle.

When you meet someone by chance or design for the first time in an open field, you should be able to find at least three things you have in common in the first minute or so, just by asking open questions, paying attention, and following pointers. In a social, safe, closed field it's even easier because you can freely add tags to your introduction and get more free information; shake hands or hug in greeting; and ask more personal questions about holidays, movies, food, traveling, clothing, music, family, sports, books, or what have you.

As kids we were terrific at bugging our parents and teachers with questions: "What's this?" "What's that?" As we grow up and gorge on the generous helpings of information and amusement the media serves up to us, the instinctive curiosity we were born with, and that got us into so much trouble when we were kids, gets rusty. Dust it off, reinvigorate it, and develop your natural curiosity. Pay attention to the world around you. Find out what makes people tick; ask for their opinion ("What do you think about that new coffee shop that opened on Main Street?"); read the paper; stay up-to-date on current events so you can give your opinion (or better still, ask for theirs) on sports, the headlines, the hot travel destinations, the new kangaroo at the zoo. Offer *sincere* compliments about the other person's tie, jewelry, after-shave, or whatever, then ask where they bought it. If the other person isn't willing to put in the effort to match your conversation level, you are not matched. If you can't find at least three upbeat things in common, it's selection/rejection time and you should seriously consider moving along to someone else.

Practice your conversation skills and become comfortable with open questions, paying attention, giving quality feedback, following pointers, looking for free information, and hunting for common ground. Make synchronizing body language and voice tone second nature in your romantic adventures and you'll find yourself natural and relaxed as you meet more and more people and chemistry starts to flow.

Now that you know how to fan the flames of conversation and synchronize for chemistry, we're going to ramp up your chemistry several notches and explore the fireworks of flirting.

the art of flirting

Flirting is more than just fun—it's fundamental. Our entire survival as a species depends on human connection. If we stopped flirting, falling in love, and reproducing we'd soon disappear. But even though nature has endowed us with all the necessary parts we need to save ourselves from extinction, not everyone knows how to use them to their best advantage. This is particularly true when it comes to flirting.

Charlene, a manager with a large clothing chain, and Kira, a physiotherapist, arrive at the popular nightclub Galapagos early enough to get a table in the middle of the action, with a great view of the bar and the dance floor. Pretty soon the crowds wander in and the place fills up. Both women are fashionably dressed and look like they belong here. As Charlene talks to Kira, she scans the room and fiddles with some loose strands of her hair. Every couple of minutes she wiggles her body and, from time to time, puts her elbows on the table and rests her head on her hands, pouting and making eyes at the male prospects at the bar. Charlene thinks she's being sexy, but she's not. She's doing what a lot of people, both male and female, do when they are out on the prowl: She's confusing being sexy with being cute. In fact, her actions only make her look insecure and childish, giving off immature energy.

Kira, on the other hand, looks poised and composed. Most of the time she sits quietly, her head lowered ever so slightly, and pays attention to Charlene. Occasionally, as she sips her drink, her eyes will peer over the top of the glass and she'll slowly take in the room. In fact, if you watch closely, Kira seems to be operating at half the speed of Charlene. She looks confident and secure and is giving off grown-up sexual energy.

Now Kira has spotted Harvey, a guy she recently saw at a party but never properly met. She'd been close enough that evening to overhear him talking about sailing in the Bahamas, and had thought he was attractive and interesting (Kira loves sailing). And now here he is with a couple of other guys, leaning against the bar. Kira keeps him in her peripheral vision and waits for him to turn in her direction.

As soon as he does, Kira counts to three, excuses herself, gets up from the table, and saunters toward the stairs up to the balcony, right past Harvey and his friends, hips subtly swaying, head slightly down. (Why the lowered head? Because we humans seem to be more intrigued by coyness than brashness.) Then Kira's eyes fix on her target for a quick moment of contact. He sees her. The second she knows Harvey has noticed her, she looks away coyly. But before Harvey has time to react, Kira glances at him again, this time closing her eyes ever so slightly as she offers a hint of a smile. Harvey gets the message.

What you just observed is what scientists call a *promise-withdraw routine* on the part of Kira and an *arousal response* on the part of Harvey. When it comes right down to it, creating excitement is all about tension and release, whether you're talking about scary movies, roller coasters, or human sexuality. The promise-withdraw routine that Kira used on Harvey is the very heart of flirting. It's used by both men and women to create arousal, and its dynamic is exactly what it says it is: giving attention,

> The promise-withdraw routine is the very heart of flirting. It's used to create arousal.

then taking it away, then giving it again—tension, release, tension; eye contact, look away, eye contact. One look doesn't necessarily mean anything, but Kira sauntered in a provocative way, gave Harvey a second look, and smiled with her head slightly lowered to suggest coyness. All this adds up to an unmistakable signal of interest. Men and women all over the world use this basic routine, based on a woman's saunter or a man's swagger, accompanied by eye contact and a smile, to signal and arouse interest in another person.

So Kira has tacitly offered an invitation and moments later Harvey responds. He comes up the stairs to the balcony where he can plainly see Kira looking down at the dance floor below. He looks her in the eye, smiles, and introduces himself. "Another drink?" Harvey asks.

"Thanks, but . . ." Kira smiles and replies, "I'm here with a friend and we're celebrating her promotion, so I really should get back to her."

"Well," Harvey replies, "You could invite me to celebrate with you. In fact, I'd be happy to buy some champagne. It's always nice to have a real excuse to buy bubbly." He grins.

Although Kira knows that Charlene wouldn't mind if Harvey joined them, she says, "That's very generous of you, but we promised ourselves a girls' night out. You know, catch up on personal stuff." She inclines her head, looking up at him briefly, then glances away.

Harvey asks, "How about tomorrow then—same time, same place, or same time, different place, or . . . ?"

Kira laughs. "Sorry, I'm not free tomorrow. But if you give me your number, I'll call you after I look at my schedule. I'm sure we can do something at some point."

The truth is, Kira knows that Charlene wouldn't care if she spent a bit more time with Harvey. Similarly, she's not that busy the following night—all she has planned is laundry. What Kira is doing is using the universally recognized *principle of scarcity* as part of her flirting strategy.

The Principle of Scarcity: How to Make Yourself More Intriguing

As a general rule, human beings want more of what they can't have, so a simple way to increase your desirability when flirting is to use the principle of scarcity. The idea is to give the impression that you are popular and in demand.

Yes, people (and even companies) use this ploy all the time, but our reaction to it is so instinctual that we never stop falling for it. For instance, everyone knows that it's notoriously difficult to get reservations at the best restaurants, but that's not necessarily because all the tables are really booked up. Similarly, fashion designers are very particular about where their lines are marketed, and their high price tags serve to exclude most buyers. When radio, television, and print advertisers bombard us with statements like "While supplies last," "Limit two per customer," "Limited edition," and "Offer good only till Sunday," they are working the principle of scarcity.

Working the Principle of Scarcity

How will taking advantage of this principle help make someone fall in love with you? By upping your "value" in the early stages of a relationship, making you seem rare, precious, and worth pursuing.

You Can't Always Get What You Want

If you could be a fly on the wall at Oggi, a popular hair-dressing salon in Kansas City, you'd be amused to hear how the receptionist treats clients, new and old alike. It goes something like this:

"Oggi, good morning."

"Hi Bethany, this is Paula Bishop."

"Hey, Paula, how are you?"

"Bethany, I need a favor. Can you fit me in on Thursday at 11:00?" Bethany checks the appointment book and sees that time slot is, in fact, available.

"Sorry, Paula, we're booked, but I can squeeze you in at 10:30 or at noon. Do either of those work?"

"Oh, thank you *so* much, Bethany. I'll take 10:30. I can't tell you how grateful I am. I'll be there on the dot."

The fact is, you'll almost never get the time slot you want at Oggi, whether that time is available or not, unless

Let's get back to our Galapagos scenario. Down on the main floor, the club is filling up. Carlos and his nephew Jason, who works in law enforcement, have just arrived and are sitting at the far end of the bar with a couple of beers. They've noticed Charlene sitting alone at the table, still pouting and staring at men she finds attractive. Her behavior doesn't specifically you book weeks in advance. Why? Because the owners have figured out the principle of scarcity. They know that when people think something is in high demand, their perception of its value increases—and that keeps them coming back for more.

The De Beers diamond cartel does the same thing. By strictly regulating the world supply of diamonds, they have managed to create the illusion that diamonds are rare and therefore worth their hefty price tag. "A diamond is forever" is a brilliant slogan, but the truth is, it is only forever because you can't get rid of it—certainly not for anything like the amount you paid for it.

When something is in short supply, or even simply appears to be in short supply, we humans feel the urge to compete for it, whether it be land, power, favor, or especially the affections of another person. Conversely (some might say, perversely), study after study has shown that whatever seems more available is perceived as less valuable.

register with them, but there is something about her that seems unsettled and rather unappealing. Their eyes move a few tables over to another woman who is also sitting alone. Dana is not fiddling with her hair in an obvious manner nor wiggling around trying to be cute. She is studying the drinks menu at her table, glancing up occasionally but not ogling the guys.

"Now there's a pretty girl," says Carlos. "What do you say? You've been single for at least six months now."

Jason grins. "Yes, she's very pretty, but I don't know. . . ." He trails off.

"Now listen, I've got this foolproof method for getting to know a girl in a situation like this. I used it lots when I was your age and it worked for me nearly every time. In fact, that's how I met your Aunt Luisa. First you spot a girl. Don't make eye contact with her; just know where she is. Walk by her once but don't look at her. Just stop and look around, then look the other way. Make sure she notices you're looking for someone, then go away. A minute later you walk up to her and say, 'I've been looking for you all over. I saw you in line (or in the crowd, or whatever) and I just had to tell you you're absolutely gorgeous. This is no corny pickup line. I just wanted to tell you you're beautiful.'"

Jason laughs and shakes his head, but Carlos continues. "No, listen, this is the real deal. At this point she might say thank you or whatever, but you just excuse yourself politely and leave. Leaving right away shows her that you're a gentleman, and you're not interested in pressuring her. It makes her feel more comfortable. Then about an hour later you spot her and make eye contact again and smile. If she likes you she'll come up to you—it really works. Don't underestimate flattery or compliments."

Jason laughs again. "Well, Uncle Carlos, I think you're right that most women want to feel like they're good-looking or smart or talented, but times have changed. My generation doesn't really believe in pickup lines. I mean, if you want to use a line, then you riff on something that's happening instead, so hopefully it sounds more natural. Even if you say 'Hi, I'm just trying to think up something to say because I really want to meet you,' that's more real and sincere than some line you got from someone or out of a book."

"Okay, maybe you've got a point," concedes Carlos. He nods in Dana's direction. "So, are you going to go talk to her?"

Meanwhile, Dana has noticed the two guys at the end of the bar who look like they are talking about her. She likes the look of the younger one. She sits up straighter, glances at Jason while lowering her head slightly, then looks away.

"I think I will," says Jason. He gets to his feet and approaches Dana. "Hi," he says. "Listen. I just couldn't help staring at you—forgive me. Can I sit here for a minute?"

"Sure," says Dana, smiling slightly. "But it really has to be only a minute."

"So why just for a minute?" Jason says as he eases his lanky frame into a chair. His tone is light and mildly flirtatious. He doesn't want to appear nosy or aggressive.

"I'm with someone and we've got lots to catch up on," Dana says, noticing that Jason didn't introduce himself. Some guys consider this a power play, but she's wise to it.

Canned Moves = Bad Moves

I don't believe in cheesy opening lines or tacky, rehearsed, smooth moves. From "I hope you know CPR, because you take my breath away" to "Is there an airport nearby or is that my heart taking off?" these ploys are totally passé. Most people are neither charmed nor fooled by any of them. Depending on the circumstances, simple questions like "Is this your first time here?" "Do you like this class?" or "I just read that book. What do you think of it?" are a thousand times more likely to work—as long as you're sincere, spontaneous, and being yourself.

Jason picks up on the tiny grain of free information Dana offered and hopes he can use it to keep the conversation flowing without resorting to the usual clichés. He continues with the light tone. "Ah ha. Does that mean you've both been having adventures lately?"

Dana laughs. "Depends on your definition of adventure, I suppose. One of us finally found a terrific apartment, and the other got a job offer she was hoping for but wasn't expecting." She glances at his eyes, then looks away.

"Hmmm. And are you the apartment, or the job offer?"

"The job offer."

"Congratulations," Jason says, smiling.

"My friend's heading back here." Dana gives Jason a warm smile.

Dana could choose, of course, to invite Jason to stay at their table, but she instead uses the principle of scarcity. Jason asks if she'd like to get together the following Friday. Coincidentally, Dana is tied up that night. Jason asks for her phone number but she replies, "I'm Dana. Give me your number and I'll call you." She has not only upped her value, but she holds all the cards in this potential relationship.

Three Types of Flirting

We can break flirting down into three main types: public, social, and private. Public flirting is usually a spontaneous, amusing, and harmless way to brighten someone's day, to add a little playtime to life or an otherwise routine relationship, and generally to spread a little happiness around. Social flirting (the kind you just saw in the Dana/Jason scenario) adds a sexual element to the mix, signaling interest. Private flirting is one-on-one, radiates sex appeal, and enhances your ability to make someone fall in love with you in 90 minutes or less. Naturally, your attitude, clothing, self-confidence, and personality all contribute to your ability to flirt but, whether you are a man or a woman, generating and sending out sexual messages through grown-up sexual energy is an integral part of making yourself more irresistible to a partner.

Personal Space

We all walk around within an invisible cocoon known as our *personal space*: The farther away someone is from us, the less threatening he is; the closer he gets, the more uncomfortable we can become—unless we've already decided to let him in.

Different cultures have different norms of personal space. For North Americans, the concentric circles of defense start roughly ten feet out (beyond which is *public space*), running from there to arm's length (*social space*), then to within arm's length (*personal space*), and finally to within a foot or so (*private space*). One of the biggest mistakes you can make during any first encounter is misjudging a person's personal space and causing his or her emotional self-defense systems to kick in. In some everyday situations (on a crowded train or elevator, when sitting in a theater or flying coach) we're able to turn off those defenses, but when we're flirting, our senses are already heightened and unexpected intrusions can be a big turnoff.

Sex appeal is what separates the men from the boys and the women from the girls. Boys and girls strive for cute, but it's the grown-up men and women, with their air of confidence, poise, and mystery, who exude real sex appeal.

Understanding the difference between cute and sexy is second nature in the world of fashion photography, especially when you're shooting attention-getting magazine covers. Cute, adorable, and sweet have their place, but there's no mistaking them for the show-stopping, magnetic pull of sex appeal. You put cute on the cover of *Seventeen;* you put sex appeal on the cover of *GQ* or *Harper's Bazaar.* Cute is for kids, teens, and baby animals. Sexy is for grown-ups.

Public Flirting

We all flirt in one way or another from time to time: cooing and playing peekaboo with a baby, teasing friends or loved ones, surprising them with small gifts or doing something thoughtful and unexpected, playing hard-to-please, acting coy, or feigning astonishment at a risqué tale. These are all playful, flirtatious behaviors designed to heighten excitement and curiosity and entice a favorable response. There are many situations where you probably don't even realize you're flirting. You banter with the woman at the pharmacy or joke with the man at the dry cleaner. The guy at the deli counter smiles and addresses you by name every time he sees you. These are the kinds of interactions humans are designed to enjoy and respond to. Public flirtation is innocent, makes us feel good (it is, after all, a form of flattery), and keeps us in touch with other people. Don't underestimate the importance of flirtation in your daily life.

Less Is More

If you've ever been to an auction or seen one in the movies, you'll have noticed that when seasoned buyers make their bids, they are very subtle with their gestures and expressions—yet their offers always get noticed. These bidders are confident, nonchalant, and slightly mysterious. The amateurs, on the other hand, are very easy to spot. They're the ones waving their hands or their programs to make sure they're seen. Take your flirting cues not from the amateurs, but from the seasoned professional bidders. Don't be pushy, don't be obvious, don't be overtly emotional, and don't go out of your way to get attention. Here, as in so many other parts of life, less is definitely more.

Fortunately, you can take advantage of opportunities to flirt almost anywhere, anytime. You can flirt for seconds or minutes, and it can happen at work, when you travel, when you shop; at church, a ball game, a music club, a funeral, a wedding, or an AA meeting. But sooner or later, you'll decide that someone with whom you've flirted deserves additional attention, and that you're interested in finding out more about him or her. That's when it's time to try some social flirting.

Social Flirting

Social flirting is a friendly and playful way to let someone know that you've noticed him and are interested, and it can signal anything from "Hi, I like your style; let's get to know each other better," to "Catch me if you can and see what might happen."

When we envision a typical social flirtation, we tend to picture two people chatting at a party or a bar or club. Both are beautifully dressed, they sip their wine elegantly, the camera cuts to a close-up of their eyes, sending unmistakable signals to each other as they make witty remarks loaded with sexual innuendo. That's great, but there are many simpler and less cinematic forms of social flirtation. It's all about making a personal connection and getting the chemistry flowing. You can use a hello or good-bye to emphasize how great things are when you're together. You can lend her your jacket if she looks cold. You can "accidentally" brush up against him, or bump shoulders casually when walking down the street. Throw a quick glance. Compliment her. Cast him a sidelong gaze. Tell her how good she'd look in that sexy dress you see in the store window.

A woman can send sexual signals by licking her lips slightly, tracing the outline of her collar with her fingers, playing with her hair or jewelry, or running her hand down her thigh. A man can do the same by straightening his tie, running a hand through his hair, or gently tossing his head.

There's obviously a fine line between too much sexual innuendo and not enough. As a general rule you should take care that your behavior isn't sending mixed signals or promising more than you're prepared to deliver. Flaunt your sexuality too much in your social flirting and you'll probably come across as a tease and/or cute or silly. Too little flaunting and you run the risk of becoming just a friend.

Flirting in Action

Let's look at an example. Genna is a naturally outgoing person who finds it easy to talk to strangers. While waiting at the Baltimore airport to board a flight to Memphis, she's spotted a guy who seems both artistic and down-to-earth—just her type. He's wearing a black T-shirt with jeans, his hair looks deliberately tousled, and his black leather bag looks worn, yet classy. He's reading a newspaper and she notices he's not wearing a wedding ring. She sits down opposite him, within his social space, and makes herself comfortable. The scene unfolds.

As she pushes her hair back, Genna "realizes" her left earring is missing. She glances down at her lap, then around her chair and under the seats next to her. The interesting-looking man has noticed her dilemma, and Genna sees that he's smiling. She has his attention. She gazes directly at him, a little embarrassed, and shakes her head. "I just lost an earring somewhere."

He offers to help, but they don't find it.

"Did you have it on when you got here?" he asks as she sits back down. He sits back down, too, but this time he says, "May I?" and takes the seat next to her. He knows that moving into someone's personal or private space can make them feel uncomfortable or even intimidated. (See box on page 202.)

"I'm not completely sure. I hope I didn't lose it at the gallery." (Note: free information!)

"What does it look like?"

Genna turns her head, moves a little closer, and brushes her hair back to show him the remaining earring dangling from her lobe.

After some small talk in which he asks her about the gallery and learns that Genna will be on business in Memphis for four days, he asks her if she'd like to meet up and do something. It's his hometown. He knows all the good spots.

She says she's not sure about her schedule but asks for his phone number. This is obviously not the first time Genna has lost an earring when she's sitting close to an attractive guy! By involving him in an amusing predicament, she's lured him into conversation, learned enough to know that she's really attracted to him, engineered a subtly sexual moment (getting close enough to show him the other earring), and maneuvered him into asking her out. Had she decided she wasn't interested

Flirting Is for Everyone

If you feel flirting-challenged, or if you feel that you're not attractive or clever or interesting enough to get away with it, don't worry. Flirting, in general, has more to do with playfulness and vitality than with broad shoulders or a pretty face. Dr. Monica Moore, a psychologist at Webster University in St. Louis, has conducted research on the flirting techniques used in singles bars, shopping malls, and places young people go to meet each other. She concluded that it's not the most physically appealing people who get approached, but the ones who signal their availability through basic flirting techniques like eye contact and smiles. Just signaling your interest in someone gets you halfway there, whether you're a man or a woman.

after all, she could have been less forthcoming or, if it went that far, turned down his offer to meet. They would have continued to talk graciously for a minute or two, then wished each other a pleasant flight and gone their separate ways.

Private Flirting

Now that we've looked at the principles behind the ancient and respected art of flirting, it's time to put those principles to work for you through private flirting. Unlike public and social flirting, private flirting is strictly about sex appeal—

not the sort that's for public consumption, but the one-on-one sort. It's about two people detecting and responding to each other's energy.

When you're with someone who may be your matched opposite and the clock is ticking, you'd better know how to flirt one-on-one and show off your sex appeal; if not, your burgeoning relationship can very easily slip into just-friends mode. Consider this next section the *Kama Sutra* of flirting.

Toning Up Your Sexual Vibes

To get to love, you have to learn how to muster and harness your sexual energy and then deliver it as part of your overall personality package. Sound daunting? Actually it's a piece of cake—or rather, four pieces, which I call *getting physical, getting grounded, eye work,* and *practice dating.*

Getting Physical

Getting physical is about getting in touch with your body through exercise—a necessity, since sexuality is deeply bound up in your physical, animal self. To be a really effective private flirt, you have to be deeply, viscerally attuned to that part of you.

You might have already gotten involved in a new physical activity as part of your socializing action plan, but if not, sign up for some classes. Even a one- or two-week program will do the trick. Skydiving, kickboxing, belly dancing, yoga,

Men Swagger, Women Saunter

Guys, if you never saw *Saturday Night Fever,* you missed the best swagger routine ever filmed: John Travolta's famous walk down the street to the Bee Gees' "Stayin' Alive." Rent the movie and buy two pairs of the most expensive, sexiest underwear you can find. (I'll explain why in a minute.) Watch the film, then put on a pair of your fancy new briefs (and the rest of your clothes!) and go for a swagger. Walk down the street, along the boardwalk, or through the mall with a smile on your face and "Stayin' Alive" playing in your head, and try to make eye contact with every attractive woman you see. Don't stop until you feel you're the sexiest guy in town. Just remember to keep it subtle.

Ladies, buy a copy of Stan Getz and Astrud Gilberto performing the song "The Girl from Ipanema" and two pairs of the sexiest, most expensive panties you can find. Learn at least the first verse by heart, up to and including, "and when she passes, each one she passes goes, 'ahhh.'" Then put on a pair of those panties and your other clothes, and go for a saunter. Take the dog for a walk, or stroll to the office or to class. As you hear the music in your mind, lower your head ever so slightly, make eye contact, and smile at those lucky enough to be blessed by your attention.

> This exercise is a must. You have to bring your sexiness to the surface if you're going to make a deep connection with another person. If you can't *feel* your sexiness, no one else will.
>
> Oh, here's why the sexy, expensive underwear: because you're going to have *The Look* written all over your face, the one that says, "I have a secret!" And I told you to buy two pairs because you're going to wear the other, brand-new pair when you go out with your matched opposite. That should keep a smile on your face!

EXERCISE

tennis, weight lifting, tae kwon do, rumba lessons—anything in which your body is 100 percent involved. Find the best instructor or association around. He or she will be your first flirt ally, helping you tune in to your own physical awareness.

If you're exercising individually, avoid distractions like watching TV on the treadmill or listening to a Walkman while you jog. Instead, listen to your body by cycling your awareness over and over from your pelvis to the pit of your stomach to your chest to your throat, and back to your pelvis. This sets your sexual energy in motion.

Getting Grounded

In the story at the beginning of this chapter, you noticed that Kira moved at half the speed of Charlene. Kira was grounded; she knew how to breathe. When you control your breath you automatically calm your nerves and relax, which in turn allows you to control your mind and your body and expand your power and energy.

There may be times when you're dating or approaching people and you suddenly feel nervous or anxious or inadequate. You want to make a run for it. This is because you've entered panic mode or, at the very least, your fight or flight mechanism has kicked in and involuntarily put you into flight mode. When this mechanism picks up signals that

To be an effective private flirt, you have to be deeply attuned to your physical self.

you are nervous or uncomfortable with a situation, it starts to pump adrenaline and shifts your breathing into your chest—so you are literally ready for a quick sprint for the hills. Unfortunately, your partner may pick up on this and also experience discomfort, and the whole thing can start to come undone. But stay calm. This is where belly breathing (or *diaphragmatic inhalation,* to give it its proper name) comes in, helping to ground you. I won't go into the vast science behind belly breathing; suffice it to say that when you breathe by pushing out your belly, your diaphragm is pulled down, which in turn allows your lungs to fill to capacity, give or take a few nooks and crannies at the top. This puts more oxygen into your blood with less effort from your heart. As a result, you literally slow down, that panicky feeling subsides, and you can resume encouraging your chosen one to fall in love with you, sans sweaty palms and shallow breath.

As well as being the most efficient way to breathe, diaphragmatic inhalation also massages your abdominal organs with every breath and improves your circulation, so get into the habit to enhance both your emotional and physical well-being. Over the next few days, whenever you can, place one hand on your chest and the other on your abdomen, and practice breathing in and out until the hand on your navel is the only one that moves.

Making Eyes

The word *flirt* in its current meaning dates back to mid-eighteenth-century England, where Lady Frances Shirley is credited with coining the term *fan flirts* to describe women who used the flitting rhythm of their fans (in combination with movements from their eyes and mouths) to tease and send sexual signals. Public use of the fan may be gone, but flirting is still first and foremost about "making eyes."

Flirting begins with the eyes because, as in most face-to-face communication, your signals go where your eyes go. After that you can flirt with your mouth (a smile, a pout), with your personality, with your shyness or your coyness, or with your sense of humor. You can flirt with words or with food and drinks. You can flirt for business or for pleasure, with goals or without. The possibilities are endless, but first you must make eyes.

Most of you know what it's like when you drive at night and shift you car headlights from high beam to low beam. They go from shining straight out in front to slightly lower down and a little more spread out, from illuminating the distance to illuminating the space immediately ahead, from dazzling drivers coming toward you to letting them know you've seen them and that it's safe to keep coming.

Flirting begins with the eyes because, as in most face-to-face communication, your signals go where your eyes go.

You can and must do the same thing when you are with your date. The most irresistible and sensual technique in flirting one-on-one is to make eye contact with your man or woman, then shift your gaze every five or ten seconds from their eyes to their mouth, then back again. This was how a fan flirt would beguile her suitors, first using the fan to hide her mouth and reveal only her eyes (as she gazed from her partner's eyes to his mouth and back again), then, while she looked him in the eye, lowering the fan to reveal her own mouth while lowering her

Looking and Loving

"Love was just a glance away," Frank Sinatra sang in the song "Strangers in the Night," and boy, was he right. A slow, deliberate gaze across a crowded room, or better still, while walking slowly toward the person, will let him or her know you're interested. Just remember we're talking *gaze* here, not a steely stare or a loony gawk.

In a study to determine the effects of the mutual gaze on feelings of romantic love, researchers at Clark University in Massachusetts had 48 pairs of male and female strangers gaze deeply into each others' eyes without looking away for various lengths of time. The subjects reported significant feelings of affection and even passionate love for each other.

eyes to gaze at his mouth. All the while she would use the gentle rhythm of the fan strokes to intensify the sexual innuendo. After a heart-stopping moment, she would cover her mouth again with the fan and bring her eyes back to his. Yow! Throw in a gentle tilt of the head at the right moment and the slightest lowering of the head and you have a loving symphony of inviting body language—all from the neck up.

Don't bother with the fan, but do alternate your gaze from the eyes to the mouth when talking with your date. It's a very, very subtle move but make no mistake: It signals sex.

You will have to practice your eye work, so choose a few people from your daily life on whom to try out these techniques. Be aware of your own body, belly breathe low and slow, synchronize your body language, and make eyes as you talk.

Practice Dating

You wouldn't go for your driving test without practicing first and you wouldn't bake an apple pie for your favorite uncle without testing the recipe, so why on earth would you go on an important date without practicing first? Here's where your next group of flirting allies step up to the plate.

Arrange two or three "safe dates" with people you feel good with: a friend, someone you haven't seen in a while, someone's brother. Just don't pick someone with whom you already have a well-established pattern of behavior, which you might slip back into without thinking. These low-stakes dates are to help you practice your new skills and evaluate what you feel good about and what needs work, but without the attendant anxiety of a real date and real expectations. The more you practice dating, the better you'll get, but two practice dates is the absolute minimum you'll need before you go on a real date with someone who could be your matched opposite. Some good places for a practice date would be a miniature golf course, a bowling alley, the zoo, a trade show, an exhibition, a pottery class, maybe even a pool hall. This type of place provides you with an activity that will help to break the ice and gives you something to talk about. You're not going to seduce the person or make them want to give up the world for you, but you are going to make them feel warm and tender towards you. Remember, ask lots of questions and share information about yourself. Look for "Me too" moments and try an incidental touch or two. Act like an adult, be aware of your body and your sexuality, practice your eye work, belly breathe, synchronize, have fun, and above all *keep the conversation and the mood upbeat and positive.*

Now He's Talking Her Language

One of the most profound ways you can be matched with someone else is through the way you both "make sense" of the world around you. We do this by taking information from the outside world in through our senses and then putting these sensory experiences into words.

In our day-to-day lives we rely mainly on three senses: sight, sound, and touch (or, more broadly, physical sensation). As we move through childhood, each of us starts without consciously realizing it to develop a favorite among our senses to help us understand the world: Some rely more on the way things *look,* some on the way things *sound,* and others on how things *feel.* Although matched opposites tend not to be matched in their primary sense preferences, here's an example of why this is important when you're making someone fall in love with you.

Where to Go on a Date?

More than anything, a date requires talking. That rules out movies, sports events, and other super noisy (or super silent) locations. When planning any real date, ask yourself these four questions:

- Is it somewhere he or she will feel safe?
- Is it something he or she will enjoy?
- Is it somewhere we can talk?
- Is it different? This is not going to be a normal event; it's supposed to be special, for both of you. Normal is easy; it's everywhere. This event needs an original context.

Keep in mind, if you've met your matched opposite, you may be remembering this date for the rest of your life. Try to make it special.

Ben has decided he can just as easily read through his notes for tomorrow's presentation at a beachfront café as he can in the office. Now he's sitting on the patio, trying not to get too distracted by the colorful parade of people strolling, rollerblading, or walking their dogs along the boardwalk. Jackie, a graduate student who comes here all the time in the spring, is at the next table cramming for an upcoming midterm exam.

When the waiter comes over, Jackie orders a double espresso and a slice of almond cake. Without realizing it (maybe), Ben orders the same thing. The waiter notices and gives a little mental shrug. When he comes back, he puts Jackie's order in front of her and says, "One double espresso, one almond cake," then moves over to Ben's table and says the same thing exactly the same way. Ben and Jackie look at each other and laugh.

Twenty minutes later the waiter returns. Ben orders another coffee and takes the opportunity to lean over and ask Jackie, "Same again?"

"Thanks. Maybe later." She smiles.

After an hour or so and a little playful flirting through eye contact and smiles, Ben and Jackie get talking. Now it's near the end of the day. Ben plucks up his courage and decides to take things a step further.

Although he's not aware of it, Ben is a *visual* person, one who's learned to respond to the world through the way things look. "Do you want to take a walk down the beach to see the sunset?" he suggests. "I love the way the sky changes color so fast, and seeing the lights come on in the cafés as it gets dark. It's such a great sight." Did you notice? Ben talks about the way things look.

"I don't know," Jackie replies. "I don't think I feel like it. I'm comfortable here for a little while longer and then I've got to go. But thanks." Did she say *feel* and *comfortable*? Maybe

Jackie can't easily relate to Ben's little sketch of the sunset. Why? Because Jackie is a touchy-feely kind of person who has learned to rely more on the way things feel, and make her decisions accordingly. Jackie is *kinesthetic*.

As we move through childhood, each of us starts without consciously realizing it to develop a favorite among our senses to help us understand the world.

Fortunately, Ben has read about the different ways people process experiences, so he recognizes Jackie's choice of words and also notices her comfortable, baggy clothes. He also notes that she speaks rather slowly and often looks down when she's thinking. The way to her heart, then, is to tell her how it'll *feel*, not *look*, to go for a walk along the beach at sunset. Ben tries again.

"You know what I like most though about walking on the beach?" he asks.

"No," she says. "What?"

"It's the softness of the sand, and the way the water swirls up around your ankles, and that sort of salty warm mist that hangs in the air around you. You know what I mean?"

Jackie tilts her head and grins. "Hmm. Now you're making me feel like I've earned a break. Why not?" She shuts her books, stuffs them into her backpack, and gives it a play-ful slap. "Hold on for a minute—I'll just go freshen up."

If Jackie had been an *auditory* person instead of a kines-thetic person, he would have noticed that her gaze tended to drift sideways either to the left or right (toward her ears) when she's thinking, or if she talks about the way things sound. In that situation, he would have done well to invite her for a walk along the beach by saying something like, "You know what I like most about walking on the beach? The sound of the waves as they break, and that gentle hiss as the surf glides up the sand, and the gulls calling overhead, and the sounds of the music as it drifts out from the cafés, and. . . ."

When you match yourself up with another person's favorite sense, you are not only talking the same language, but also seeing through the same eyes, hearing through the same ears, and feeling through the same feelings—and that can be a powerfully seductive thing.

Which description of the walk along the beach did you most easily relate to?

How to Identify People's Sensory Preferences

Visual people are the snappy, impeccably tailored folks who dress to impress and judge others by their appearance. Visuals make quick decisions but need to see evidence. They frequently look up to the left and the right when looking for answers to questions. A visual person may wave his or her hands around when talking and have a fast-paced, monotone voice that seems to come from high up in his or her body. Visuals use picture language, saying things like "I see what you're saying," "That looks good," "Do you see my point of view?" "That idea isn't clear," "I'm hazy about that," "My mind went blank," "Let's try and shed some light on the subject," "We need a new perspective," "I view it this way," "The way I see it . . ." and "Looking back on it now. . . ."

Auditory people are often relaxed and stylish in the way they dress. They have more melodic, smooth, fluid, and expressive voices that come from the chest area. They gesture somewhat less than visuals, and may look from side to side (toward their ears) when thinking about what they'll say next. Auditory people favor sound language, saying things like "I hear you," "That rings a bell," "Sounds terrific," "Everything just suddenly clicked," "Listen to yourself," "Something tells me to be careful," and "I can really tune in to what you're saying."

Kinesthetic people are all about feeling and physical sensation. They care about comfort in their clothing and surroundings. While many kinesthetic folks tend to have somewhat fuller figures, you'll also find many athletes are kinesthetic. They have slower speech, easy-going voices and gestures, and tend to look down when they think about

Don't Try Too Hard

In a study conducted at Princeton University, students of both sexes were questioned about their methods of sizing up people when they meet for the first time. Overeagerness was one of the most reported turnoffs. Don't smile too hard, don't try to be too witty, don't be overpolite, and resist the temptation to be patronizing. If you're putting on an act, you'll come across as a phony. Sure, be friendly and smile, but avoid having a grin on your face all the time. People who don't know when to stop smiling and grinning end up appearing insecure and foolish.

what to say next. Kinos make decisions slowly, pay attention to detail, and speak in physical language, using phrases like "It just feels right," "Let's get a handle on things," "Do you grasp the concepts?" "I'm up against the wall," "Hang in there," and "I can't put my finger on it, but I have a feeling you're right."

Remember, Flirting Is Fun

Some people are born to flirt, others have natural flirting skills that seem to come and go depending on the circumstance, and some of us just have no clue and need to be taught—but we all have the potential. Flirting can move a regular pleasant conversation to a different level or create an air of expectancy that says, "It's just the two of us." You can flirt with your eyes, your mouth, your body, your voice, your sex appeal, your words, and any of your senses.

Public flirting is just a question of attitude—you don't have to be intense about it. Every day you come in contact with people left, right, and center, whether you're at a bar, on the bus, or at a pottery class. So make eye contact, smile, and go over and say "Hi" if it feels right. Social flirting revolves around a promise-withdraw routine and is a playful way to signal that you're interested in someone. Private flirting is about intensifying playfulness and sexual overtones as you make that special someone fall in love with you. If you flirt with panache and subtlety, you'll make yourself irresistible.

9 creating intimacy

Up until now, we've devoted a fair amount of time to understanding the unspoken signals that convey trust, comfort, and respect: eye contact, a sincere smile, open body language, physical feedback, and synchronizing—because you'll never get intimate with someone quickly unless you can establish nonverbal rapport. We've also spent some time learning how to talk to someone in a way that lets you find common ground. Now we're going to take conversation to a deeper level and use it to prepare the way for intimacy.

Straight for the Heart

A good old heart-to-heart talk, with you and your partner both opening up and discussing your experiences, your ideas, your hopes, dreams, and feelings, is the single best way to create emotional intimacy. The closeness and trust you share evolve into that wonderful "just the two of us" feeling that's the cornerstone of a loving relationship. It creates understanding and unity, and quickly leads to love and bonding.

At the heart of creating intimacy is self-disclosure. Basically, self-disclosure is revealing intimate information about yourself—your experiences, your ideas, your hopes, dreams, and feelings. It's not a one-way street, though. The goal is that your partner offers the same kind of information about him- or herself, just like the couples in Dr. Aron's experiment did (see page 4). You reveal something personal about yourself, then he or she reveals something personal about him- or herself. The simplest way to encourage this return of information is to synchronize your body language and tone of voice, and give feedback. Synchronizing builds trust and comfort, and feedback lets the person feel as if he or she is truly being heard.

Emotional intimacy has two main components: risk and commitment—the former because you're opening yourself up, the latter because as you open up together you become intertwined emotionally. Think of your hands and your fingers. When your fingers are closed, all you can do is place your hands together, but when your fingers are spread, your hands can become intertwined and strongly bound. In this chapter you're going to learn how to open your emotional fingers with your potential partner and become intertwined. Part of the process is that you each take turns. Self-disclosure is an invitation to trust. There are levels of risk involved, but the greater the risk, the deeper the trust.

Lies and the Lying Liars Who Tell Them

Tell lies and you're doomed. I can't tell you how many people I've heard tell outright lies about themselves when getting to know someone new. They're rich and own several businesses. They're about to sign a record deal. They're friends with Michael Douglas. They're 29—really. This kind of behavior happens in both real-world and online dating, and is one of the worst things you can do. Sooner or later, the person you're trying to impress comes face-to-face with the truth, and then it's all over. No second chances.

Generally speaking, *low-risk* self-disclosure is personal information that a good friend will probably know about you—your likes and dislikes, how many siblings you have, and light-hearted stuff from your past and present, such as your hobbies and pastimes, your favorite board game, the silliest thing you ever bought. "I'm happiest when I'm tinkering with my car." "I'm always forgetting birthdays." "I can't tell a joke to save my life."

Medium-risk is personal information you don't normally reveal and trust to just anyone—your opinions, your dreams and aspirations, good and bad judgments or choices you've made. You might reveal what you did as a kid that got you in the most trouble, the one food you could eat every day, your favorite ways to escape reality. "When I was younger, I dreamed of being a professional tennis player, but when it came down to it, I realized I didn't have the drive." "I came here on vacation three years ago and never left." "What I'd really like to do is quit my job and go raise horses in Montana." These kinds of revelations will help you both get a fuller sense of your compatibility. You'll be able to tell whether it's worth spending more time with this person and if there is real opportunity for mutual trust.

High-risk self-disclosure is visited only occasionally on a first encounter. It involves trusting and sharing your deepest feelings, and even your fears and insecurities. "I sometimes wonder if people find me interesting." "I'm the black sheep of the family." "I'm too old for games." High-risk usually requires that you change the upbeat tone of low-risk and medium-risk disclosure to a more serious key. While high-risk can lead to deep trust and bonding, it's not called high-risk for nothing. Think hard before you reveal things that might be a complete turnoff to someone who doesn't yet know you well. And remember, you're not just going to say this sort of thing to anyone—you are building deep rapport and encouraging emotional invest-ment in someone who might just end up being your matched opposite.

A Few Ground Rules

When you feel the time is right for self-disclosure, it can help to have a few things in mind rather than blurting out the first thing that comes to you. Remember, your date is still in select/reject mode too, and you still need to be charming, not alarming. Come up with three or four things you think he or she would understand and perhaps feel the same way about. When the time is right, reveal one and see where it goes. If the response is good, you can go on to the next one, taking turns sharing feelings and ideas.

Since there is risk involved in this kind of self-disclosure, here are a few ground rules.

1. *Move cautiously and considerately, paying close attention to the feedback you receive.* The flow should be natural and easy—no surprises, no shock value statements, and the mood must remain upbeat.

2. *Judge your topics.* Sharing *experiences*—trips you've taken, adventures you've had, and the like—is probably the least threatening form of self-disclosure. Sharing *ideas* involves more risk since the conversation can get heated if you get into politics, religion, and values. Sharing *feelings* is the highest-risk kind of disclosure, so be sensitive and moderate yourself according to your sense of how shy the other person is.

3. *Take turns.* When one of you reveals something, the other must respond in kind. When talking with a friend, it's not always necessary for him or her to respond to your ideas, experiences, hopes, and feelings. In self-disclosure, however, you're asking your date to reciprocate. Handle it like a game of tennis, taking turns, cementing what you have in common, and determining how much you really are like one another, one revelation at a time. As you finish speaking, look away briefly. This signals that you're done. When you look back at your date, you're inviting him or her to speak—and he or she will.

4. *Pace yourself.* In a way, the process of self-revelation is like an emotional striptease, but nobody is going beyond their undies. You don't just back up your confidential truck and dump everything out at once. There's only so much most people are prepared to reveal about themselves early on, and there's only so much you want to hear from the other person.

Getting Too Personal

Self-disclosure is the key to intimacy, but there's a fine line between baring your soul and unloading your baggage. Stay away from anything embarrassing or socially inappropriate. This is not the time to mention that you spend $100 a week on lottery tickets, or that your mother is a kleptomaniac, or

Conversation Jitters

Sometimes being nervous can cause you to talk too much, or not enough. If you feel nervous, stop and call it something else—*excited* sounds much better. A few moments of belly breathing can calm you down, then you can turn your excitement into a smile, saying to yourself, "Hey, am I ever excited. This is *great*."

how difficult it is to buy shoes with bunions like yours. And you probably already know this, but it's worth repeating: Stay well away from discussing your previous dating and sexual entanglements, at least until you are fully committed to each other. And even then, tread lightly. A discussion of your romantic past can quickly slide into comparison, competition, and insecurity.

Keep in mind the principle of scarcity and play your cards one at a time—a little mystery is good for love. Talk too much and you deflate the mystery, inflate your vulnerabilities, and end up appearing pitiful, boring, and definitely not sexy. On the other hand, if you talk too little, sooner or later you'll stop being mysterious and just become hard work. You may even come off as arrogant or aloof and seem just as boring and unsexy as the person who doesn't know when to shut up.

A Conversational Road Map

If you look carefully at a couple as they become absorbed with one another, there's a pattern to what happens. Their movements and voice characteristics become synchronized. There's plenty of eye contact, smiles, open body language, gazing, private flirting, and great attitude. But there's also a detectable pattern to the way the conversation flows. It goes something like this:

1. *The conversation starts with small talk. Small talk* is light or casual conversation about nothing in particular. A good place to start this chitchat is with an occasion/location statement followed by an open question, as you saw in chapter 6. The weather, the news, or sports will do in a pinch—just don't linger on them too long.

2. *Very early on, the small talk gets blended in with play talk. Play talk* is anything funny or playful, from an amusing observation about the location or occasion to something funny that you've seen, read, heard, or experienced recently. Late-night TV hosts use play talk all the time—check out how they do it. Engaging in play talk will give you an idea of your date's sense of humor and attitude toward life.

3. *And after a while, it shifts into the higher gears.* Using small talk and play talk as a base, the conversation shifts at a certain point through low-risk, medium-risk, and (very occasionally) high-risk self-disclosure.

Talk Show Teachers

If you want to learn more about conversational patterns, watch talk shows and notice how adept the hosts are at keeping conversation moving. Leno, Letterman, Conan O'Brien, and Oprah are particularly good. Try to identify the classes of talk (small, play, low- and medium-risk). Pinpoint when the shifts between these types of talk take place. Most of the late-night hosts (I'm not talking about the serious interview folks here) shift from small to play talk in the first five to ten seconds with a new guest.

These shows are free tutorials that can help you learn and practice the art of conversation right in your own home. But keep in mind that the self-disclosure on these shows is not mutual, it's one-sided. It's all about getting the guests to open up. The host is there as a facilitator. There are occasional exceptions, though, like the time on *Late Night* when Julia Roberts turned in her chair so she faced Letterman rather than the audience. She deliberately synchronized herself with him, gazed unwaveringly into his eyes, then teased him through a seductive self-disclosure session, telling things about herself and getting him to reply in kind. He was visibly flabbergasted at the energy she cooked up between them right there on the air.

EXERCISE

Getting Ready to Reveal

In preparation for changing the tone from just friends to something more intimate, think about the kinds of things you might reveal. It can help to write them down. Put them in a journal or notebook so you can review, amend, and add to them from time to time.

Low-Risk Disclosure

* What could you say about your likes and dislikes, without getting too deep?

* What lighthearted anecdotes can you talk about from your past and present?

* What amusing stories could you share about family, friends, hobbies, or your hometown, school, or work?

Medium-Risk Disclosure

* What could you share about your opinions, your personal feelings, your dreams and aspirations, your plans for the future, your good and bad judgments, or choices you've made?

High-Risk Disclosure

* What will you need to share (when the time is right) in order to have a better chance at intimacy and closeness?

* What can you say about your deep feelings, your fears and insecurities, your understandable human weaknesses?

Remember to look out for a "Me too" moment, which can take your conversation to another level. That moment can and should come very early on, during play talk or even in small talk. Watch for it, because as soon as it happens, that's your trigger to move to low- and medium-risk self-disclosure. The "Me too" trigger means you've gone from first gear to second in terms of intimacy.

Walking the Talk

Mario attended one of my early workshops on making someone fall in love with you. One day out of the blue, I got an e-mail from him: "I feel I must thank you for the success I am having in my life. It all started when I took your workshop in Toronto. Your advice saved me from going down the wrong path. I have since found my matched opposite and am having a great time. I would love to have a coffee with you when your schedule permits. Thanks again, Mario." A few days later we met and he told me his story. I have taken some license with his words to help make the story more useful, and as you can probably guess, Mario is not his real name.

Shy, Cautious, and Reserved People

What can you do if the person you are with is reluctant to talk about him- or herself? You can synchronize. There is no more powerful way to open someone up than by synchronizing body language, voice characteristics, favorite words, attitude, breathing, and timing. This will get you into his or her mood. Take it easy, ask gentle questions, and be patient. More than likely the person is kinesthetic, so speak his or her language. Remember Jackie from chapter 8's section on sensory preference? She was kinesthetic and Ben got to her by talking about the way things *feel* rather than how they look or sound.

If you are the one who's a little shy or reserved about revealing yourself, start off slowly—or even better, practice with a friend. Tell him about your vacation or your work; tell her about your hometown or your favorite restaurant. Just describe things that you find interesting. When you start feeling more confident you can start putting more of your personality into it, adding opinions, perhaps about a book, a movie, or the headlines in today's paper. Once you can do this comfortably, try telling someone how you feel about him or her.

First, a little background: Mario is 29. He started his own toy company when he was 22 and got rich quickly after inventing a toy that became a bestseller. Soon he had two new toys that were also doing well, but the once fun-loving toy inventor quickly became all work and no play, putting in 18-hour days. He had trouble meeting women, and when he did meet someone he found attractive, he tried to use his expensive car and fancy clothes as a shortcut to connecting. Now he's ready to try my method.

Mario has met Amanda several times in the coffee shop next to his office, where he goes every day for an extra-large coffee or latte. A few times, they've bantered good-naturedly about which flavors they prefer. Having attended a few of my workshops, Mario has gotten pretty good at getting free information, so he's learned that Amanda works as a physiotherapist in a sports injury clinic and that she's an amateur competitive cyclist.

Mario likes Amanda's energy, her warm smile, and her athletic build. He feels good around her and suspects they could be matched opposites. He wants to ask her out.

More than anything, as I've said, a date requires talking, so Mario rules out movies, sports events, and other super-noisy (or silent) locations. As he filters his ideas, he asks himself the four questions from the last chapter:

- Is it somewhere she'll feel safe?
- Is it something she'll enjoy?

• Is it somewhere we can talk?
• Is it different?

He doesn't want it to be a normal date—he wants it to be a special event for both of them. Normal is easy, it's everywhere. He wants this event to have a romantic context.

Mario Makes His Move

Mario decides to ask Amanda to cycle down to a festival on the waterfront. His choice fulfills all four conditions, and has the added bonus of not requiring his BMW, so he'll get a sense of whether Amanda likes him just for who he is. (All Mario has told her is that he's in the toy business, not that he's the inventor of the Super-Slugger Bongo Bat, the third-bestselling toy in North America that holiday season.)

Mario has also carefully thought out *how* to ask Amanda. Here's what he says: "How about a bike ride down to that street festival on the lakefront this weekend? I haven't ridden my bike in months so you'll have to slow down for me, otherwise you're gonna be seeing me at the clinic instead of the coffee shop."

Mario followed certain guidelines in coming up with his plan. By deliberately adding common ground (bike riding) and a hint of humor (his physical condition), he softened the question and made it easier for Amanda to say yes. Romance needs encouragement at the start, so the *way* you invite someone out is as important as the nature of the outing itself. The more fun, exciting, and unique you can make your invitation sound, the greater the chance of the invitee accepting it.

The Date

Mario arranges to meet Amanda at a downtown square where families take their kids to feed the birds. Before they set off, they engage in some small talk.

"It feels so great to be out on a day like this," says Amanda.

"It sure does," he answers. "I just love the sun on my skin. Hey, nice bike," he adds, looking at Amanda's fancy mountain bike. He then turns to face her, smiling, pointing his heart at her heart, and making sure to keep his body language open. "I'm relieved," he says. "You didn't bring your racer."

She grins, already unconsciously synchronizing with him, then looks at his bike. "Yours isn't so bad, either. Shimano brakes, good derailleur—I thought you said you weren't very serious about riding."

"Hey, I was going to ride my tricycle, but then I got brave and took out the two-wheeler."

Amanda laughs and gives a mock bow. "Well, I'm honored." They've definitely moved from small talk to play talk and Mario's having fun, so he decides to reveal something personal but not too risky. "Seriously, though," he says,

"I feel great on a bike. I love the wind in my face, and the sense of sailing along under my own steam."

Amanda's eyes light up. "I know what you mean! I'm really happiest when I'm riding." She has just responded with some low-risk self-disclosure of her own. They mount their bikes and set off.

Down at the waterfront, they lock up their bikes and stroll toward the festival grounds. Mario, who normally walks at a laid-back pace, picks up Amanda's brisker walk. "Hey, look at that!" he says. They pause to join a crowd surrounding two guys on unicycles juggling three eggs, a frying pan, and a lit butane torch back and forth between the two of them. Somehow by the end they have three fried eggs in the pan, and are still on the unicycles. "Pretty amazing," says Amanda. "You know, I've always wanted to learn how to ride a unicycle. It's supposed to be really hard."

"No kidding? Me too!" Mario can't believe he's gotten in a "Me too" moment so quickly and easily. He really *has* always wanted to learn.

"Are you serious?" Amanda leans towards him slightly as she says this and looks directly at him.

"I am. Of course, I've always wanted to learn how to fry an egg as well."

Amanda laughs, but Mario notices that she's no longer leaning toward him; in fact, she's looking away. Oops. He

Asking for a Date

Take a few minutes to think about what, if anything, you know about your date.

- Where did you first meet?

- What do you have in common?

- Where can you go that would be unique and memorable while offering a comfortable environment for conversation?

- Where can you go that could incorporate your shared interests?

Now consider your choice of words. Think about:

- How to bring up common ground or shared interests

- How to keep your request light and casual by interjecting humor

- How to soften the request

List a few ideas for what you might say when you ask for a date.

realizes too late that although the joke was funny, the timing was wrong. Here Amanda had just willingly revealed a little dream of hers, he'd moved things toward greater intimacy with the "Me too" moment, but then he'd pulled the dialogue back by cracking a joke.

But maybe he can recover from it. He looks at her. She's now watching a stilt walker who's approaching in the distance. Mario figures maybe he'll gamble with some low-risk self-disclosure of his own. "It's true, you know. When I was a kid I used to love the circus, all of it, but I got a special kick out of the clowns on unicycles."

Amanda looks back at him. "How come?" she asks, as if testing to see if he's serious or just a clown himself, the kind of guy who constantly makes jokes—and that's all he does. The wind whips a lock of hair into her eyes and she pushes it away.

Mario says, "Well, I don't admit this to many people, but. . . ." He casually brushes hair off his forehead as he says this, mirroring her gesture. "I was a real klutz. The last kid on my block to learn to ride a two-wheeler. Seven years old, still had the training wheels on." Mario has just revealed a more serious soft spot; he's moved into medium-risk territory now.

Amanda looks at him sympathetically. "That couldn't have felt good."

"You got that right. I got teased real badly. So the fact that the clowns could do that with only one wheel seemed like magic. Not to mention dangerous. They were always acting like they were going to fall off. And, of course, I thought it was all 'real' danger so I was doubly impressed." Amanda smiles again and Mario notices that her shoulders have seemed to relax ever so slightly. He makes sure his are relaxed as well.

"I remember the first time I ever went to the circus," she says, finally. "I was really young, like three or four, and I cried through most of the clown acts because I thought they were really hurting each other when they bopped each other on the head and stuff. My mother says all the other parents were staring at her like she was some sort of abusive parent, because her kid was bawling and all the others were hooting and hollering." Amanda is grinning as she says all this, and shaking her head as though at her own silliness, but then she quickly looks down and nervously tugs at her hair again.

Mario can see that Amanda is feeling vulnerable and a little embarrassed about revealing this particular soft spot. "You must have been a pretty sensitive kid."

"I guess."

"Did you get teased about it a lot?"

"All the time. My two brothers were the worst. They used to see who could make me cry the fastest." Amanda is looking at the ground as she says this.

Mario feels genuinely moved and vows *not* to play the clown. "Aww," he says gently, and then lightly, quickly, touches her arm. "That's so mean."

Amanda looks up again. She seems genuinely grateful that Mario understands. "Anyway, I'm a big girl now."

They gaze at each other for what seems like a long time. Mario looks into her eyes, then down to her lips, then back to her eyes. Then he blushes beet red and Amanda gives him a huge grin.

"So big girl, want an ice cream?" he says as a pushcart vendor goes by. "It's getting really hot." Sensing that Amanda is shyer about personal disclosure than he is, Mario has decided to throw in some small talk for a few seconds, to keep things from getting too heavy or threatening.

"Sure," she answers, grinning, "but only if they've got chocolate. I think vanilla's just a waste of calories."

"I'll second that," Mario says, grinning back—another "Me too" moment! Amanda seems genuinely at ease now, so, as he hands her a chocolate ice-cream cone, he says, "You know, I can really relate to your clown story. Not only was I a klutz, but I was a sensitive kid too—it was really easy to hurt my feelings. I think I got over that part, but I'm still a klutz." Another soft spot revealed. He hopes that won't turn her off. She's clearly not a klutz if she competes in bike races.

But no, she's still smiling at him. "You don't seem klutzy to me," she says.

Ah ha! thinks Mario, *That sounds pretty positive.* Then Amanda's eyes catch something in the crowd. "But even if you are, that's okay," she adds mischievously, "because I still cry at clowns!"

Mario laughs and follows her gaze. Two guys in polka-dot suits and red noses are coming down the path toward them, waving balloons. So they're back in play talk mode again,

Mario notes, and he's happy to go along. Plenty of time later for more low- or medium-risk self-disclosure. He really likes Amanda. He's having more fun than he's had in months. He feels pretty sure they're clicking. "Quick, run before they start hitting each other!" he yells, grabbing her arm, and they hightail it, giggling and hooting, toward the next attraction.

Why the Date Is Going Well

So far, so good. For the first few minutes Mario and Amanda engaged in small talk and play talk, just chatting playfully for its own sake and to discover more about their interests and what they have in common. Once they arrived at the festival, they began to chat about what was going on around them, and from there moved on to childhood memories.

At least that's how this normal, innocent conversation appeared on the surface. What happened

> **Mario purposely revealed personal information about his own life to encourage certain reactions and responses from Amanda.**

beneath the surface is that Mario purposely revealed personal information about his own life to encourage certain reactions and responses from Amanda. Mario also very gently synchronized his body language, voice tone, and choice of words with Amanda's, and before long he steered the play talk into low-, medium-, and possibly (from Amanda's point of view) high-risk self-disclosures. Yes, he made a misstep with the egg-frying joke, but he recovered, used the incident as feedback, and was still able to take the conversation from casual to intimate, at which point he used some private flirting eye work to show off his sexuality. He was careful not to make another joke after Amanda revealed a more serious soft spot. And, because he now knew she was somewhat shy and sensitive, he steered the conversation back to more neutral small talk (offering ice cream) to avoid giving the impression he was crowding or interrogating her. His strategy worked, because after he then revealed another soft spot, she felt safe and relaxed enough to come back with a fairly high-risk intimate disclosure by making a joke (about crying at clowns) at her own expense.

Incidental Touching

If the process of creating intimacy has three gears and the "Me too" trigger gets you into second gear, then incidental touching can boost you up into top gear.

The persuasive power of touch has been the focus of lots of research. In one experiment at a library, a slight brush of the hand when patrons handed over their library cards was enough to improve that person's opinion of the library. Another experiment showed that if a waitress touches a patron just briefly when she returns his or her change, her tip will be about 15 percent higher than normal. Learning institutions know that if a teacher momentarily (and appropriately) touches a student, it is likely to result in a better understanding between them.

The active word here is *incidental.* This means natural and almost accidental. Grabbing, fondling, pawing, and all other form of gratuitous groping are the kiss of death. Incidental touching is done with the hand and is brief, gentle, natural, and nonthreatening. You may touch the person's arm or shoulder but never anywhere that's overtly sexual (the breast, the butt, the inner thigh). This first touch is like a magic wand that can only be used once with full effect.

Choose your moment with care. Too early and you are a pawer. Too often and it has no impact. Too late and the moment has gone. Your first incidental touch should come around the time you are comfortable with medium-risk self-disclosure—preferably after you have laughed together and leaned in to each other.

If your well-timed and brief touch on the arm prompts a warm response, you can follow it with an appropriately-timed, incidental touch to the hand. But beware: You are in his or her private space. If this passing touch isn't reciprocated with an increased sense of intimacy, back off immediately or you are toast. If it is reciprocated, go to a deeper level of intimacy. By now, the self-disclosure should be flowing easily. Wait a short while, then test the mood with another brief yet more deliberate touch to the hand. This may turn into a gentle hand squeeze, perhaps even a *momentary* handhold.

The Complete Pattern

Here's what the whole conversational routine looks like when you add in the triggers:

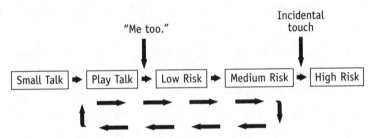

Deeper Self-Disclosure

Let's watch another scene unfold. See if you can identify the conversational stages as Elaine and Robert pass through them.

Elaine is a Boston primary school teacher in her early forties. Three years ago, after 14 years of marriage, her husband left her for a woman who's ten years younger than she. Elaine's self-confidence took a big hit, but she's trying to gain it back because she likes being in a relationship and hopes to find another life partner. She's determined to approach potential relationships differently.

Robert is an architect. Never married, he's had two long-term, live-in relationships but has been single now for almost two years. Elaine and Robert met at the dog run a few months ago, and now they make it a point to look out for each other. She finds him attractive and easy to talk to. In one conversation, she mentioned that she doesn't have a car, and Robert offered to take her out of the city some weekend. Now Elaine has gathered up her courage and decided to take him up on his offer.

Elaine Makes Her Move

"I've heard that the village of Marblehead has some fantastic antique stores as well as some pre-Revolutionary buildings. Maybe if we went there you could teach me the difference between a gable and a lintel. "Oh—" She smiles here— "And show me a pilaster while you're at it. I've always wondered what the heck a pilaster is."

As Mario did with Amanda, Elaine has chosen a date that includes common ground, is safe, is different, and will allow them plenty of opportunity for conversation, and she's framed it using some light humor. Robert laughs when she mentions pilasters and happily agrees.

The Date

In the car on the drive down, Elaine and Robert engage in small talk about the weather and their dogs, both of which are contentedly curled up in the back of Robert's station wagon. "Looks like it's going to be a great day," says Robert. "Look at that sky."

"I'm glad it's a bit cool, though," Elaine adds, "because the dogs will be okay in the car when we go into the shops."

"Yeah, they'll be fine. And there's a conservation area just outside of Marblehead where we can let them run."

"Well, I wouldn't call what Bertie does 'running,'" says Elaine.

Robert chuckles. Bertie is Elaine's laid-back and slightly overweight basset hound, whose long, heavy body and stubby legs don't exactly make him a sprinter. "Well, he's soulful, and hey, his legs reach the ground. That's all that matters."

Elaine laughs. "Bertie and Clara together make a pretty funny couple." Clara is Robert's elegant, long-legged Weimaraner. "People will think she's only with him for his money."

The small talk and play talk continue as they drive into Marblehead; then, as Robert parks the car, he says, "I'm thinking of adopting a greyhound from one of those greyhound rescue organizations. They get them from the racetracks."

"Really?" says Elaine. She sits up straighter and turns her head to look at Robert as he turns off the ignition and faces her. "I just read an article about one of those groups, and I almost phoned them up yesterday to do the same thing. I couldn't bear the thought of so many of those dogs being destroyed simply for lack of homes."

He looks up at her. "You did? That's amazing!" He rubs his chin thoughtfully. Elaine suddenly realizes that what just happened was a "Me too" moment, and she didn't even have to work at it. Elaine casually mirrors his gesture, and she too touches her chin lightly as she says, "As a matter of fact, I have two rescued cats at home that I got from a cat rescue group." This is a bit of very low-risk self-disclosure, or so Elaine thinks.

"Hey, you didn't tell me you had cats!" says Robert. He gives her a mock look of disapproval. "You're supposed to be a dog person!"

He says it lightly, but Elaine feels that suddenly the connection has been broken. Maybe Robert really hates cats? She has to find out. "Well, of course, I'm a dog person," she says, throwing a fond glance at the snoozing Bertie, "but I'm a cat person too."

"But cats are sooooo not dogs!" exclaims Robert. "They're so unaffectionate and self-centered." There's some kind of soft spot here—more like a little patch of quicksand, thinks Elaine, judging from the intensity of Robert's reaction.

"That's—" Elaine, who has a bit of a quick temper, is about to say "That's ridiculous!" but stops herself just in time. Instead she decides to choose a more upbeat attitude and play it more calmly and diplomatically. "That's what a lot of people think," she says, keeping her voice pleasant. They're out of the car now, and standing side by side on the sidewalk, but Robert's body language seems somewhat closed, his arms tight at his sides. "In fact," continues Elaine, making sure she's now facing Robert, heart pointed at his heart, "I used to be like you—I used to hate cats!"

This is medium/high-risk self-disclosure, but it seems to have done the trick, probably because it also included common ground. "I never said I *hated* them," says Robert, his posture softening. "It's just that every cat I've ever met has either snubbed me, used my briefcase as a scratching post, or peed in my boots."

"Ah," murmurs Elaine as they begin to walk down the main street, "the true origin of the Puss 'n Boots legend!" Robert laughs. Good. A little play talk can't hurt here, she figures.

"So how did you go from hating to owning them?" asks Robert.

"We always had dogs growing up," says Elaine, "and my parents didn't like cats, so I didn't either."

"Hmm," says Robert. "Just like my family. We always had dogs too. My dad thought cats were nuisances."

"But," continues Elaine, "one day a cat chose me. Just showed up on my porch yowling in a huge snowstorm. I'm not heartless, so I put a box with blankets on the porch and gave it some food and water. Well, it just purred and purred and rubbed up against me."

"They do that when they want something." Robert's expression is amused, but Elaine can tell he's still not convinced.

"But this one did it all the time! Fed or unfed. He just won me over. He loved to cuddle in my lap and followed me around the house like a dog! And when he died, I was heartbroken. It happened around the same time some other things were going badly for me. . . ."

Elaine considers mentioning her husband leaving her, but decides that information is too high-risk at this point in the relationship. This is not just a soft spot, it's a sore spot, so instead she'll use something medium-risk. ". . . And I have to admit I was at a pretty low ebb. Then I saw an ad for a cat rescue group. I called them, and the next thing I knew I had two tabby kittens. And you know what, you just can't stay depressed with two kittens in the house."

"Well, I agree that kittens can be cute. The trouble is, they grow up to be cats." Robert laughs, but his head is tilted away from Elaine.

She can't believe he's so closed-minded about cats! Something else must be going on with him, and she wonders if it's too early to probe. Closed-mindedness in any area makes Elaine nervous, so she wants to find out more. "Hey, it sounds like maybe you had a bad experience with a cat in a past life or something," she says lightly, as they pause to look in an antique store window.

"Well, as a matter of fact, you're right." Robert's voice drops and he looks away from Elaine. "That cat that peed in my boots belonged to my ex-girlfriend. I swear she loved that cat more than she loved me. She was totally neurotic about it, and the cat was neurotic too." *Ah ha,* thinks Elaine, *now we're getting somewhere.* Robert has just revealed a sensitive area!

"Let me see if I can figure this out." Elaine drops her voice a little as well. "Animals are pretty sensitive, you know that. The cat was probably jealous, especially if you didn't try to make friends with it. And let me guess: It was a male, and it peed in your boots when things were going badly with your girlfriend."

Robert looks at her and laughs. "Exactly right! You must be psychic."

"No, I just know cats. They're much more complicated than dogs."

"You mean like women are more complicated than men?" Robert's tone is slightly challenging, but he's grinning and looking relaxed.

Elaine grins back. Play talk is good for now. "Hey, I didn't say it! But relatively speaking, dogs are simple and cats are complex. Attention and food—from just about anyone—that's all dogs are about. Much as I love them, I don't find them very discriminating or subtle."

"Kind of like men?" Robert asks, his eyebrows shooting up.

"You know," Elaine says, smiling and raising her eyebrows slightly as she briefly touches the sleeve of Robert's jacket, "complicated can get exhausting. A lot of the time I just want simple."

They both start to laugh, and Robert takes a deep breath. "You're funny," he says. "I like that in a woman. Even one with cats."

Why This Date Went Well

If you look back, you'll notice that from the get-go Robert set an upbeat tone, saying, "Looks like it's going to be a great day." Elaine picked up on that and ran with it in her practical way: "I'm glad it's a bit cool, though, because the dogs will be okay." As their lighthearted remarks about the two dogs' looks ushered in some play talk, Robert moved into low-risk self-disclosure with free information about adopting a greyhound. Elaine was so stunned at the coincidence that she didn't entirely capitalize on a superb "Me too" moment. Saying "Me too" lets you inject magic. You can pause when you deliver it, punctuate it with a shift in voice tone or attitude, and in this case she could have even touched his arm "incidentally."

Nevertheless, she did let him know they had some very specific common ground. Whether it was conscious or not, the discovery of this common ground had Elaine synchronizing herself with Robert as she touched her chin and told him about her cats. This turned out to be high-risk and not very well thought out, since many people equate a pet's characteristics with its owner's—not a good thing considering Robert's low opinion of cats.

Hats off to Elaine, however, first for controlling her temper, second for picking up on her faux pas, and third for a superb attempt to realign herself with Robert using open body language and her little "I used to be like you" speech.

These mildly strained moments are bound to happen. Elaine inadvertently upset the balance and was gambling that her mixture of animal logic and human emotion could get them back on track. Luckily, she was able to get Robert to volunteer information that explained the reason for the tension. It worked. Robert was beginning to see the intelligent, patient, and caring side of this schoolteacher, and he found it appealing. And Elaine was seeing the kind, reasonable, and slightly vulnerable side of this architect, and she found it very comforting.

It's a Matter of Perspective

Who said 90 minutes is not much time to get to know someone? True, if you *um* and *ahh* and fill the space between pregnant pauses with small talk and shallow pleasantries, it's not enough time. Likewise, if you ramble on and

Turn Awkwardness into Opportunity

If you accidentally stumble into a delicate area with another person, use the information as important feedback. Tread lightly, probe gently, know when to back off, and synchronize like mad to reassure the person that you're sensitive and trustworthy, and aren't going to use the information in any harmful way.

bore each other to death, or sit there and say yes and no and make no effort to truly converse, it can seem like an eternity. And if you are rude or shifty or bossy or pretentious, your date will want to stop the clock at 90 seconds and make a dash for the door.

But when you find common ground, pay attention and share your thoughts; you are going to know a lot more about each other after an hour and a half than you did at the outset, and will likely be able to say, "I feel like I know you so well. Where did the time go?"

If you're with someone you really like and you've let the real you come through, using your body, your attitude, your voice, and your words in a natural and easy way, you have prepared the ground for love.

If you have spent 90 minutes with a matched opposite demonstrating that you like each other, you have prepared the ground for love. If you have used your body, your attitude, your voice, and your words in a natural, easy way to engage in mutual self-disclosure, you have created emotional intimacy. If you have found "Me too" moments, touched in a natural way, and spent some breathtaking moments gazing into each others' eyes, then you have planted the seeds of true love.

getting to love

True love is a unique blend of attraction, intimacy, commitment, and romance. It's utterly personal and happens a little differently for every couple. For some, the moment it strikes is easy to pinpoint; for others, it's less obvious. Some notice a definite moment when suddenly everything changes; for others, it's more of a flow, a gradual tide of change. Emotional people tend to admit love more quickly than their more rational counterparts, even if the seeds were sown at the same time.

So how do you get from intimacy to love? Up until now I've offered very concrete techniques. These techniques —adopting a great attitude, flirting, synchronizing, self-disclosure—will bring you to the brink of love, and often beyond. The momentum of two people coming together and discovering they are matched opposites is frequently enough to carry them through to love. But if we're going to discuss how to turn an inspiring attraction to and connection with someone into true love, we need to move away from the practical step-by-step approach into a more philosophical realm.

If You Love Something, Set It Free

There's a beautiful Taoist saying that I urge you to reflect on for a day or two. It goes, "Free from desire, you marvel at the mystery. Caught in desire, you see only the manifestations." It's about not judging things by the way you expect them to be.

When you know what you want and have done all that you can to get it, step back and allow events to unfold. If you do this, you'll get more than you could have ever imagined. But if you try to force your desire, all you can see is whether you are getting it or not. It's like trying to force an egg to hatch or a flower to bloom. Instead, you must let go and let life and love transpire in their own creative, surprising way.

> Love doesn't happen on command. It's a process that flows, it's a seed that grows, it's a spark that turns into a flame.

It's about having faith in yourself, in life, in the person you love. Love is infinitely more surprising and exciting than you could ever imagine—but only when you give it the room, the support, and the opportunity it needs to unfold. Love doesn't happen on command. It's a process that flows, it's a seed that grows, it's a spark that turns into a flame. All you have to do is try to be ready for it—put your best self forward, then let go and marvel at the mystery.

Mario and Amanda

Let's go back and see how love happened for Mario and Amanda.

"We said goodbye promptly at 6:00," Mario told me. "I was a bit troubled because toward the end of the date Amanda started to change. She was getting irritable and impatient as we got closer to saying goodbye. But we'd clicked. I could actually see it in her eyes. It was like her soul had opened up and I could fall right inside her through her eyes. We told each other what a great time we'd had, but she was acting more and more nervous and excited at the same time, so I took your advice: I didn't force it or jump to conclusions. I asked her if we could meet again. Then she floored me. 'Not for a week or so,' she said. It took my breath away and it must have shown. She promised to call me. We hugged—well, actually she hugged me real tight and said, 'It'll be fine,' and off she rode. I wanted to feel crushed, but I didn't go there—thank goodness.

"The next three days were awful. Then on Thursday at work, by absolute fluke, I happened to be at a window overlooking the parking area and I saw someone slip something under the windshield wiper of my car. It was Amanda. I shot down the stairs a flight at a time and flew out the side door, but she'd gone. Hell, was I ever shaking. As I walked quickly over to the car, I was thinking I must have been hallucinating because even if she'd figured out where I work, there's no way she'd know my car. But there was an envelope taped under the driver's side wiper. Inside was a gift certificate from the coffee shop where we met. On the back was handwritten one word and a phone number. The word was 'When?'

"*Now,* I thought. *Right now, this moment.*" Mario sat back; he had almost finished his story.

"Anyway, I called, and the rest is history. We met again, it was bliss, we're married, we're mad about each other, and we're having a baby in December."

I congratulated him and we chatted about family life and kids for a few minutes, but then I had to ask him a question. "Back up a second. The last thing I heard before all this was you were ready to feel crushed."

"On our date, Amanda told me she'd been seeing this hockey player, not exclusively, but certainly for quite a while. When we got together she told me she had wanted to deal with that before we met again." We talked a while longer, and Mario told me a waiter at the coffee shop had pointed out his car to Amanda so she could leave the note. Then he and I said our good-byes. I agreed that Wendy and I would be there for the baby's christening.

Mario knew the seeds had been planted, he knew they'd clicked, and he knew everything was in place, but he also knew not to interfere with the natural flow—even though it hurt like hell. Sometimes you have to simply trust that everything will work out and just let go. By setting things free, you allow them to align themselves in perfect time.

Elaine and Robert

Elaine and Robert both longed for companionship but after experience with failed relationships were more cautious than Mario and Amanda. Elaine in particular had been bruised by the unraveling of her marriage and now found herself single and lonely. She longed for the companionship and security that came from being with someone special, but she wasn't about to leap into anything before taking a good long look. Robert, too, was treading lightly; he regarded his two unsuccessful relationships as personal failures. Still, despite their cautious outlooks, both realized they had found something special in one another. They could laugh together, run with their pets together, and talk together.

Elaine confided, "When we first got talking at the dog run in the park, I remember thinking, 'Where did the time go?' It was like that every time we met; there was never enough time. Robert made me feel it was okay to dream again. He's very organized and he got me thinking straight—my life seemed to add up to something more than just the day-to-day routine I'd got stuck in. On our second date he told me he felt sparks

Along with the thrill of new love comes the potential for heartbreak.

fly—nice bit of medium-risk. That really woke me up. I'd never have guessed by the way he acted. I almost told him that's the kind of thing I thought I'd never hear again, but that would have been too high-risk for me. Still, we took it slowly. We dated for six months before talking about love, and two more after that before talking about moving in together."

After almost a year of friendship and more than ten months of dating, Robert and Elaine moved in together. Two years later they pooled their resources, relocated, and opened an antiques shop in Rockport, not far from Marblehead, where they spent their first date. Today they are inseparable.

Some folks are more cautious than others. Along with the thrill of new love comes the potential for heartbreak. Some people choose blithely to follow their heart and hope for the best; others want to be sure that they're on solid ground before throwing their lot in together. Both attitudes have their merits—it all depends on your circumstances. The main thing is to be open to love, to allow it to happen in a way that feels comfortable for you.

Love at First Dance

If Elaine and Robert are examples of people who took their time making sure their relationship was strong, Larry and Anita represent the opposite approach. Both were members of a singles club for people who enjoy horseback riding. Larry was working his way up the management side of a record company, and Anita ran the reference library for a law firm.

Every Sunday the club put on a cowboy singles night. One of the rules at this event was that the women invited the men to dance and the men weren't allowed to refuse. One Sunday night in September, Anita invited Larry to dance—twice. Anita sensed some real chemistry, and so did Larry. They left the dance separately, but both returned the following week. This time Anita invited Larry to dance three times, the maximum number allowed. During their last dance Larry asked Anita out for lunch, and she accepted.

Larry chose his date well, asking himself the four questions from chapter 9—Is it somewhere she'll feel safe? Is it something she'll enjoy? Is it somewhere we can talk? Is it different?—and came up with an idea for a unique, special, romantic occasion. He arranged for them to meet at the stable where he boarded his horse, rent a mount for Anita, and then ride a trail through forest and meadow to a lakeside restaurant that welcomes riders. It's about two miles from

Actions Speak Louder than Words

Truly matched opposites can fall in love in 90 minutes or less, given the opportunity to build trust and achieve emotional intimacy. That doesn't mean they come right out and say it as the clock strikes 90. Some do—they process their feelings into words, then thoughts, then actions quickly; they are emotional and spontaneous. Others take longer to process their experiences into words and want to live with a feeling for a while before expressing it. When you find your matched opposite (or he or she finds you), the seeds of love are there waiting to be triggered. Don't expect to say or hear "I love you" in the first 90 minutes if it's not in your (or your partner's) nature to articulate feelings so quickly.

the stables to the edge of the forest, where the restaurant sits between the pines and a lake.

In Anita's memory, they had a perfect date. "Lots of conversation and chemistry," she told me. "After we got back to the stables we untacked the horses and brushed them down. It must have begun with the brushing and the smell of the horses and the sound of Larry's voice. I could hear him talking gently to his horse as he ran the brush along its neck. I got this floaty feeling of well-being. Everything was peaceful and where it should be. I don't know if that makes sense."

It's enough to know that profound sense of well-being, of trust, of happiness, of relief.

If you don't want to articulate your feelings, you can look for the telltale physiological signs that what you're experiencing is mutual. Are his or her pupils dilated? Face flushed? Breath a little shallow with excitement?

Falling in love triggers changes in the body as well as the mind. The sexual impulses that shoot up the spinal cord into the brain stimulate involuntary contractions and relaxations of muscles. The body releases dopamine, endorphins, estrogen, oxytocin, norepinephrine, and testosterone. The glowing complexion, the excited breathing, and the dilating pupils are physiological indicators of sexual arousal.

"Perfect sense," I said.

"As we walked up the path to our cars, I could still hear the horses in the distance and smell the lake. Larry stepped aside to let a truck go by and as he did his hand brushed against mine. It felt very big, where he touched me, and very deep. I got this warm rush up my arm—to my heart, I guess," Anita continued. "Then I did something that was so out of character for me but so natural at that moment. I stopped and put my hand on Larry's arm and said, 'Can I ask you a question?' He raised his eyebrows, nodded, and gazed at me—right inside me. I swear he knew what I was going to say next. 'Does it get any better than this?' He didn't say anything for a few moments, then he let his breath go and smiled. All he said was, 'Oh, my.' Then I heard myself say, 'Where are we going with this?' He looked confused so I added, 'You and me.' It was easy; it just seemed like the right thing to do, a sort of epiphany. Then Larry said, 'How about married within a year?' All I could do was laugh and say, 'Holy cow!'"

That was nine years ago. Today, not only are Larry and Anita happily married, but they run a successful market research company and work, commute, travel, socialize, and play together.

Keeping Love Alive

Love is not a destination, it's a process, a journey. But how do you keep your love alive and special throughout that journey? Through romance. You make gestures to show him he's the most important thing in your life. You pay attention to her and take action to show her the romantic fires are burning. Romance is the art of expressing sentimental love. At its simplest, it is amorous gestures toward the one you love; at its best, it is deliberately creating wonderful memories that serve to form a foundation on which you build the loving relationship of your life. The key to successful romancing is through the senses. Remember visual, auditory, and kinesthetic (page 217)? Play to the preferred sense of the one you love.

Martin asked Shelley if she'd mind coming along to a local marina with him after work one evening. He had to deliver something to a friend who was sailing in from across the lake that afternoon. He picked her up and they drove together. Martin took a soft canvas sports bag out of the trunk and they walked over to the transients' dock, but Martin's friend hadn't arrived yet. He suggested they sit on the dock, dangling their feet in the water. As they sat in the sun on the gently rocking dock and waited, Martin said, "You know this is the exact spot where we met a year ago?"

"Yes, I know." Shelley replied, and wrapped her arms around him. After a few seconds Martin unzipped the canvas bag. Inside was a bouquet of yellow roses, a bottle of champagne, two glasses, and a plate of hors d'oeuvres. "There's no friend," he confessed, smiling. "Happy first anniversary."

• • •

Antonio, who ran a small art gallery, had met Susan, a teacher, almost a year ago when he'd gone with a group of friends to a performance by the Mexican National Ballet Company. Since then, Mexico, Mexican food, and all things Mexican had become romantic notions for them.

One sunny afternoon, as Susan led her class out of a field trip to the National Gallery, she saw Antonio waiting on the sidewalk, holding a "Happy Birthday, Susan" sign across his chest. With him was a five-piece mariachi band that he'd hired, trumpets and all. Susan is auditory; she is especially moved by the way things sound. That was 15 happy years ago.

• • •

Hats off to Gerard for the unforgettable way he popped the question to Dina. After a romantic dinner at a lakeside restaurant on Georgian Bay, he took her out in a rowboat to watch the sunset. Just as the sun was sinking below the horizon, he presented Dina with a ring and asked her to marry him. There were tears and hugs as she said yes. Dina didn't notice the flashlight Gerard had in his hand. As they hugged, he surreptitiously switched it on and waved it toward the shore. It was the signal for three of his friends to set off the $220 worth of fireworks he'd brought in, lighting up the sky and reflecting off the lake around them. What a sight it was. Dina is visual—she can be especially stirred by the way things look.

• • •

Romance is probably the opposite of common sense, but sometimes it's worth throwing practicality aside to show the one we love how much we care. The best romantic gestures require thought and effort. (What does an e-mail greeting card say about the sender's commitment and resourcefulness?) But that thought and effort are usually well worth it in terms of keeping the relationship vibrant and happy.

Jeanette blew all her savings to take her race car enthusiast boyfriend to see the Monte Carlo Rally. They are getting married next year. Kayla had seven wild pairs of boxer shorts delivered to her boyfriend by courier on Valentine's Day, when he was away on tour.

Think of your love as a fire you must tend with enthusiasm every day. Each of you needs a pile of logs. Those piles don't have to be the same size, but over time you both have to contribute to keep the fire glowing. When the flame burns bright, it brings warmth and happiness and you can play in its glow, but if you take the fire for granted, it'll go out and you'll be out in the cold, alone. Feed the fire every day. You can give flowers or other surprise gifts, rent a favorite film, read to each other, write little love notes, or just have a cup of tea ready when one of you arrives home on a rainy day. The possibilities are endless. Keep your fire burning brightly.

Putting It All Together

Love happens differently for everyone, but the process is the same. Find your matched opposite, plant the seeds, water them, and watch them bloom. Or, make some sparks, create a flame, and keep it burning—whichever metaphor works best for you.

To get to this point you're going to need to use all the techniques and skills you've learned, so let's review them.

Everything begins and ends with attitude. It's what people respond to even before they meet you. You can choose your attitude just like you choose your clothing. And remember, not only does your attitude drive your behavior, it affects the behavior of the person you're with too. You can use your attitude to signal *I'm nervous, I'm shy,* and *I'm aloof,* or you can use it to signal *I'm fun, I'm confident, I'm available,* and *I'm here.*

Dress to be your best self, the you that's happy, confident, resourceful, and ready to meet any challenge. Your clothes send a message. The better you dress (and I don't mean more expensive, but rather well coordinated, well fitting, well maintained, and stylish), the better the quality of attention you'll get and the better you'll feel about

> **Nothing says trust and approachability like eye contact, a smile, and open body language.**

yourself. Sex appeal comes from attitude and body language, for sure, but it also comes from the pants, skirts, shirts, blouses, shoes, and accessories you choose, as well as the way you do your hair.

Socialize and entertain. Your matched opposite is out there. Finding him or her is a numbers game. Get out and meet as many people as you can. Ask friends and coworkers to make introductions. Focus on improving your social skills and cultivating your friendships. Get involved, make plans, follow through, be friendly.

Use your body to signal you are open and trustworthy. Be charming. Nothing says trust and approachability like eye contact, a smile, and open body language. Of all the parts of your body you can use to transmit signals of attraction, the eyes are by far the most important and capable of the most subtlety. Use them to convey your interest and to create intrigue. Look into your date's eyes for a few seconds, then to his or her lips, then back to the eyes.

Flirt socially. Hold eye contact a little longer than normal, look away, then look back. Men and women, the more you move with poise and grace, the more interesting you appear. Women, you can also use your body to promise and withdraw, to say *I'm available—maybe.* Guys, get in touch with your male energy and learn to swagger. Women, get in touch with your female energy and learn to saunter. Not in a way that's over-the-top, but just enough to let people know you've arrived and you are confident.

Create chemistry and rapport with your conversation and your synchronizing skills. Appeal to your date's preferred way of taking in the world (Does he or she talk more about the way things look, sound, or feel?) and find common ground. Nothing helps build good feelings like synchronizing body language and voice characteristics.

Make your date a romantic and memorable special event. Make it somewhere you can talk and your partner will feel safe, something he or she will enjoy, and something beyond the everyday.

When the moment comes, flirt privately. Crank up the sexual vibes with your words and your body language, especially with your eyes. Get intimate with play talk, small talk, and self-disclosure. Exchange truths and confidences in your tête-à-tête to create emotional intimacy. Synchronize, relax, enjoy, and move your relationship to that beautiful feeling of mutual clicking. Look for "Me too" moments and touch incidentally.

Be romantic. Romance keeps a loving relationship alive. The next time you see one of those couples that seem to be crazy about each other—the ones that act like newlyweds, but you know they've been together for years—check out how they interact. I'll bet they romance each other every day.

Romance doesn't just make you feel good in the moment. It creates memories for the future—memories that bind, memories that elate, memories that energize, memories that keep you young at heart, memories that make *your* love special and unique, and storybook-like memories that make your relationship together worth hanging on to and fighting for in the tough times.

it all begins with you

O nce upon a time, you couldn't swim, and swimming didn't make sense. You thought, "If I take my foot off the bottom of the pool, I'll sink." But you'd seen other people swimming, so you knew that even if it seemed impossible, it could actually be done. At some point your imagination worked with you instead of against you, and eventually you learned how to swim. Now you can do it without thinking, as naturally as a fish.

Once upon a time you couldn't ride a bike. You thought, "If I put both feet on the pedals, I'll fall over." But what the heck, you had faith that it was possible because you saw others doing it. Once again, your imagination spurred you on and now you can ride that bike without thinking. It's as easy as pie.

With both swimming and bike riding, though, you had to practice. At first you couldn't float; at first you couldn't balance. And then, one magical day, you realized no one was holding you up in the water, and no one was steadying the bicycle. You were swimming or pedaling all by yourself, moving freely and confidently under your own steam.

It's the same with finding your matched opposite. Once upon a time, you couldn't figure out why some people appeared to sail through life and have amazing relationships without seeming to try and you couldn't. But that was once upon a time. Now you have faith in the methodologies you've embraced in these pages because they make sense. You've seen other people find their soul mates and you know that the magic moment will come for you, too.

Just as with swimming or riding a bike, though, you can't really learn how to fall in love from reading a book, not even this one. Sure, you can read about the different swimming strokes or the parts of a bicycle; you can learn the theory and physics behind the sport. But to really get to the heart of the matter you've got to leap in and learn by doing.

So it is with love. I went out and looked at what's going on when people find and remain deeply in love, and I put what I learned in this book. I've talked to people who consistently got relationships wrong and had to learn from their mistakes. I've given you the theory, I've given you the techniques, but if you want the chemistry, you've just got to make the leap and start practicing. Mere wishing or hoping you'll find the person of your dreams isn't good enough. No matter how persuasive or optimistic you are, you have to get up, go out into the world, and have some experiences. And that's where faith comes in to motivate you—faith in yourself and faith that the person who's going to sweep you off your feet and keep you buzzed forever is out there and will find you when you least expect it.

It all begins and ends with your self-talk, the way you explain to yourself what's happening around you. Focus on the positive and you'll get it. Focus on the negative and you will get that, too. Remember, as your experiences become words, your words become thoughts, your thoughts become ideas, your ideas become actions, your actions become habits, your habits become your personality, and your personality becomes your destiny. If true love is to be in your destiny, you must embrace and accentuate the positive. The moment will come when you realize you've found someone you click with so well that love just unfolds—as naturally and easily as swimming across a pool or cruising on a bike. Are you ready? I'm letting go of your hand. You have all the tools you need to ignite the flames of love in your life—I've given you the kindling, the firewood, and the matches—but only you can light it. You're on your own now and you'll be fine. When love comes, it will come as a surprise. It always does—out of the blue. That's part of the dizzying mystery of love and the giddy rush of romance. So go ahead and strike up a match—and be ready for the best surprise of your life.